newbery on the net

Reading & Internet Activities

Second Edition

Ru Story-Huffman

UpstartBooks

Fort Atkinson, Wisconsin

Elizabeth,

This one is for you.

Love,

Your Mommie

Published by UpstartBooks
W5527 Highway 106
P.O. Box 800
Fort Atkinson, Wisconsin 53538-0800
1-800-448-4887

© Copyright by Ru Story-Huffman, 2002
Cover design: Frank Neu

The paper used in this publication meets the minimum requirements of American
National Standard for Information Science — Permanence of Paper for Printed
Library Material. ANSI/NISO Z39.48-1992.

Contents

Introduction

Often we must mix elements of the past and present with the tools of the future to make sense of our surroundings. One such rich and creative mixture is the combination of the Newbery Medal books and the Internet. This mixture combines the traditional literature approach to learning with technology. As a combination of literature and technology, *Newbery on the Net* is a resource for teachers, librarians, and parents who wish to use literature as an aid in exploration of the Internet.

With little doubt, children have long read and loved Newbery Medal books. As a staple in elementary classrooms and libraries, the Newbery Medal books are steeped in history. Established in 1922, the John Newbery Medal is awarded each year to the author of the most distinguished children's book published in America. Presented by the American Library Association, the Newbery is named in honor of John Newbery, an eighteenth century English bookseller. Winning the Newbery, which is announced at the American Library Association Midwinter meeting, is a very high honor.

These great stories are often included in the elementary and middle school curriculum. Addressing universal themes of childhood, educators using the whole language and balanced reading program methods of teaching find rich rewards for their students in their use. Newbery books have been used to teach social understanding, friendship, history and many other lessons from life. Libraries also use the Newbery Medal books in their programs for children in elementary and middle school.

In *Newbery on the Net*, we expand the appreciation and study of these great books through the use of the Internet. The Internet provides access to the World Wide Web (WWW), a development that has changed the face of our educational system. No longer is the Internet considered a "new" technology. In fact, more homes, schools, businesses, and people have come to rely on the Internet for information and entertainment and to aid in research. State and local education boards have implemented technology standards into curriculum, and studies have been completed on the impact of technology on learning. The combination of the Internet and Newbery Medal books leads to a discovery of learning, much like the Internet itself. The Internet can be viewed as a web; at the center of the web is the learner. In the learning activities included in this book, the learner will travel different routes or use different links to discover specific information. Along the way, information literacy skills will be enhanced, students will be exposed to many other pieces of information, and they will have the opportunity to use creative learning to locate, disseminate, evaluate, and synthesize information.

How to Use This Book

Through the use of *Newbery On the Net*, children will be exposed to quality children's literature and the wonders of the Web. Blending literature and electronic resources, educators and librarians can expand learning opportunities for students. The activities here have been developed using the WebQuest concept, which was developed by Bernie Dodge at San Diego State University.

A WebQuest is an educational activity that uses the Internet to teach children. It is a web page that contains specific tasks, questions, processes, and Internet links. Children are provided a scenario and have stated educational activities to complete their goals.

In *Newbery On the Net*, I have taken the WebQuest concept and expanded it into a model I call the LearningQuest. Educators who do not have the time or resources to mount a web page will find this guide offers many creative options. Libraries or schools that do not have the necessary computer hardware to satisfy a group learning experience can use the LearningQuests in paper format. The LearningQuests included here are designed so that students can read from the reproduced pages of this book and do the Web search using the recommended Internet URLs (Uniform Resource Locator) or links. The links chosen for inclusion in *Newbery On the Net* have been chosen to best comply with educational standards for children.

Using LearningQuests in the Library & Classroom

Twenty-four complete LearningQuests are included in *Newbery On the Net*. Each is a complete, ready-to-use instructional resource that can be used for either individual or group study. Each contains a concise introduction, a clearly written assignment, current Internet sources that can be used to complete the assignment, questions that provide further enrichment, guidance and helpful hints to aid students in the completion of the assignment, a conclusion to further reinforce the objectives of the lesson, and further notes for the teacher or librarian.

The age level for the LearningQuests is upper elementary through middle school. However, the reading level of the Newbery books varies, and we recommend that you refer to the reviews and publishers' recommendations for a more precise estimate.

It is intended that the LearningQuests are to be mounted on your school or library website using any standard HTML (HyperText Markup Language) editing software. If you lack time or sufficient library, computer lab, or classroom computers to do this, you may also reproduce them directly from this book for library or classroom use.

Two templates for the LearningQuests are included in the back of this book (p. 102). One is a text version to illustrate the recommended standard format. This template identifies where the information in the 24 LearningQuests should be inserted. The second template contains the HTML codes that you can apply. The HTML template is also available on the web page created for *Newbery On the Net*, and it can be downloaded from *http://www.hpress.highsmith.com/rshup/template.htm*.

WebQuests

WebQuests were developed by Bernie Dodge at San Diego State University. For more information, you might try the web page created by him for WebQuests at:

The WebQuest Page
http://edweb.sdsu.edu/webquest/webquest.html

There are many additional sites with further information:

WebQuests: What Are They?
http://education.nmsu.edu/webquest/index.html

WebQuests in Our Future: The Teacher's Role in Cyberspace
http://school.discovery.com/schrockguide/webquest/wqsl1.html

WebQuests in Our Future: A Slideshow
http://www.school.discovery.com/schrockguide/webquest/wqsl1.html

A WebQuest About WebQuests
http://edweb.sdsu.edu/webquest/webquestwebquest.html

Some Thoughts About WebQuests
http://edweb.sdsu.edu/EdWeb_Folder/courses/EDTEC596/About_WebQuests.html

Using WebQuests in Your Classroom
http://pd.l2l.org/linktuts/inteweb.htm

WebQuests Handout
http://gilligan.esu7.k12.ne.us/~esu7web/resources/webqhand.html

WebQuest Resources
http://gilligan.esu7.k12.ne.us/~esu7web/resources/webq.html

WebQuests
http://www.spa3.k12.sc.us/WebQuests.html

WebQuest Template
http://www.esu7.org/~esu7web/resources/wqtemplate.html

Many Internet sites have WebQuests which have been developed by educators. To access available WebQuests on the Net, use the keyword "webquests" in your preferred Internet search engine.

Introduction

The templates can also be used for additional LearningQuests you may wish to develop. In addition, many other WebQuest templates can be found. If you are interested in further exploring the use of WebQuests, the sites on the previous page offer a number of good sources for information and activities.

Computer Literacy

It is assumed that children in the upper elementary grades and middle school possess basic computer and Internet skills sufficient to use the LearningQuests. *Newbery On the Net* is intended to further strengthen these skills, while stimulating reading interest. The *Information Literacy Standards* prepared by the American Association of School Librarians (AASL) and the Association for Educational Communications and Technology (AECT) provide a framework and goals for improving student use of computers, the Internet, and other educational technology.[1] This book was written to contribute to these goals through activities that are clear, understandable, and enjoyable.

I offer one important warning: Students must be trained on how to use Internet browsers before attempting a LearningQuest. Establishing a basic level of computer skills will also aid in the utilization of this volume. An overview of the basic skills needed to ensure students will be able to work successfully through the LearningQuests is provided on p. 9. This second edition includes LearningQuests for the 1999–2001 Newbery Medal winners and the most up-to-date websites for all topics.

Website Evaluation and Selection Criteria

The Web has many "authors" including educational institutions, governments, private industry, profit and nonprofit corporations, and everyday people. It is within these pages that the learner is exposed to all types of information. Critical thinking is an important tool for students to possess. The Internet can aid in the development of critical thinking, higher order reasoning and discrimination of sources. Deciding authenticity of information presented is important when using the Internet to educate and entertain children. When librarians, teachers, and parents choose literature for children, they use certain criteria to aid in that selection. When finding Internet sites for use in an educational setting, having an understanding of the information presented is very important. To aid in the selection of Internet resources, the following concepts should be considered before any website is recommended for students to use.

Authorship: You can get some ideas about authorship from the domain name, but often finding the real source of the information is difficult.

◆ Is the author or authoring organization provided? Who is the "author" of the Internet site? It is a college or university? Government? Corporation? A personal homepage?

◆ Is the source of the information given? (This information should be available from the site author on request if it is not given on the site.)

Working with New Computer Users

If children are unfamiliar with computers and the Internet, the following steps are recommended:

Introduce the students to the following basic computer skills, either individually or in small groups. Demonstrate each step, and then ask each student to repeat them. Stress the importance of seeking the assistance of a teacher or librarian if they forget these procedures or they experience any problems.

- How to turn on the computer.
- If the computer is password protected, review the use of the password and the reason for security, as well as the computer log-on procedure.
- Explain the computer's menu, and what the icons represent.
- Demonstrate how to use the computer's mouse to access specific programs.
- Demonstrate how to exit a program, log-out, and turn off the computer.

The next day, ask the students to repeat these procedures. Continue to repeat this process until each student has mastered these basic steps.

After the students have mastered the basic computer skills, introduce them to the Internet and the World Wide Web, using the following steps:

- Explain that the Internet is a network of computers, and that the World Wide Web provides access to a "library" of information resources. Note that a browser permits a computer user to locate and access specific "sites" or pages on the Web, and that each of these pages has an "address" called a Uniform Resource Locator (URL).
- Show the students how to use the computer's modem to access the Internet. Explain that a modem is required to access the Internet using telephone lines. If a password and specific log-on procedure is required, demonstrate how that is done.
- Once you have connected to the library's or school's Internet Provider using the computer modem, demonstrate how to locate a specific website using the computer's browser.
- Be very careful to explain that not every website on the Internet is appropriate for children, and they should only use URLs that have been recommended for them, such as the Web sites included in this book.
- Let them search for specific sites using sample URLs contained in this book. Explain the importance of using the exact URL, and demonstrate what happens the URL is incorrectly keyed.
- Demonstrate how to log out of the Internet and exit the modem. If your school or library does not have unlimited access to the Internet, explain the importance of logging in and out as soon as the search has been completed.

Repeat this procedure on the following day, and on succeeding days until all students have mastered these basic steps.

Introduction

Purpose: Each site on the Web has a purpose for existing, these include informing and educating, but also selling, persuading, and misinforming.

- Does the page provide a statement about its sponsorship and purpose?

- Is there advertising? Does it detract from the other site content?

- If authorship and purpose are not stated, is there a bias in the presentation?

Content: Answers to the questions above will help to evaluate issues of bias and quality. Some other issues to consider about the content include:

- Does the Internet web page meet the needs of stated educational goals, curricula, and standards?

- Will the information contained educate and entertain the children?

- Is there too much information presented which may frustrate the young learner?

- Is there information included which does not pertain to your subject, or would be harmful in some way to children?

- Is the Internet page age appropriate for the audience? Is it too advanced for the intended grade or age level.

Currency: A major problem with the Internet is obsolescence. Websites have a tendency to disappear. Information found on Internet web pages can be relevant one day and outdated the next. Or you may be looking at information that hasn't been reviewed or updated in a couple of years.

- When was this page last updated? Is the information presented out-of-date? Was new information added at the last updating?

- Are there any inactive links included in the Internet sites? If you find links to other information that are inactive or outdated, you can assume the initial site has not been thoroughly checked.

Design: Consider the overall design of the page for information clarity and presentation.

- Has the site been designed so that you can move through it easily and quickly to find the information desired?

- Is the page fun to use; will children find the presentation stimulating or entertaining when visiting the page?

- Are there too many graphics, or are the graphics so large the page is slow to load?

- Is the page hard to decipher?

Ease-of-Use: A web page that is difficult to use may provide a frustrating experience for children and adults.

- Is the Internet site easy to search?

◆ Is the search engine or mechanism easy to manipulate, or do they pose possible problems for children?

Evaluation Resources

Evaluation of Internet sites is a growing concern. The Internet itself features some evaluation criteria websites. To further your understanding of the criteria used in selecting web pages for educational use, visit these sites:

Critical Evaluations Surveys

http://school.discovery.com/schrockguide/eval.html

CyberGuides: A Rating System

http://www.cyberbee.com/guides.html

The ABC's of Website Evaluation

http://school.discovery.com/schrockguide/ppoint.html
Choose "ABC's of Website Evaluation" in the PowerPoint format to view a presentation developed for educators on web page evaluation.

Selection Criteria

http://www.ala.org/parentspage/greatsites/criteria.html

Evaluating Web Resources

http://www2.widener.edu/Wolfgram-Memorial-Library/webevaluation/webeval.htm

Teachers' CyberGuide

http://www.cyberbee.com/guide1.html

Internet Curriculum #3: Evaluation of a Web Page

http://school.discovery.com/schrockguide/brush/intles3.html

The Good, the Bad, and the Ugly

http://lib.nmsu.edu/instruction/eval.html

As with any information, careful evaluation can save time and energy and provide the best learning situation possible. Evaluation of the Internet and the information presented will aid in the instructional design for all computer-aided instruction.

In Summary

Children are exposed to computers at a very young age. *Newbery on the Net* is designed to introduce computer skills, increase awareness of information, and entertain children. At the same time, children will be exposed to quality children's literature, which can aid in the development of necessary reading skills.

Although *Newbery on the Net* stresses the Internet and educational technology, literature is a vital aspect of this volume. The Internet exposes children to new ideas, thoughts, and information. As do books, which have long been a part of our lives, and will continue to influence us. Through books, children and adults have been educated,

Introduction

entertained, enlightened, and enriched. We use books in a variety of situations, and Newbery Medal books represent children's books held in high esteem by children and adults. Those who use *Newbery on the Net* in the classroom, library, and home have the opportunity to continue the time honored tradition of quality literature, accompanied with the resources of the electronic frontier.

Notes

1. American Association of School Librarians/Association for Educational Communications and Technology. *Information Literacy Standards for Student Learning.* Chicago, ALA, 1998.

Newbery Medal

Introduction

The Newbery Medal is awarded each year to the author of the most distinguished children's book published in America the previous year. Winning the Newbery Medal provides recognition for writing achievement and is a high honor.

Assignment

As you complete this LearningQuest, you will discover information about the Newbery Medal. You will learn about the history of the medal and the criteria for choosing an award-winning book. You will use the World Wide Web to answer questions about the Newbery Medal and books which have received this award.

Internet Resources

Your media center or public library has a collection of Newbery Medal books. Select and read some of these stories. Also, the World Wide Web has some good Web pages which feature the Newbery Medal.

The Newbery Medal
> http://ils.unc.edu/award/nhome.html *Activities 1 & 2*

The John Newbery Medal
> http://www.ala.org/alsc/nmedal.html *Activities 3 & 4*

Welcome to the Newbery Medal Home Page
> http://www.ala.org/alsc/newbery.html *Activity 5*

Past Newbery Medal Winners and Honor Books
> http://www.ala.org/alsc/newbpast.html *Activities 6 & 7*

Activities

1. Who is the Newbery Medal named for?

2. Who proposed the idea of awarding the Newbery Medal? When?

3. Who awards the Newbery Medal?

4. How is the winning book chosen? What are some criteria for choosing the award-winning book?

5. What is the title of the most recent Newbery Medal book?

6. What is the title of the Newbery Medal book for the year you were born?

7. What are some titles of other Newbery Medal books?

Additional Activity

Once you have found the answers to your questions, be prepared to share your findings with the class through an oral presentation. In addition, use the site below to find a review of a Newbery book you have read:

> **The Orange Grove Review of Books**
> http://www.cfsd.k12.az.us/~ogwww/reviews/ogre.html

Search by author or title.

1. Read the review and prepare a synopsis of the review to share. Include: Title, author, grade of the reviewer, whether the review was positive or negative, and if you agree with the reviewer or not.

2. Prepare a book cover for the title of the Newbery Medal book you reviewed.

Conclusion

Newbery Medal books are read by many children throughout the United States. Now that you know about the history of the Newbery Medal and how it is awarded, try to decide if a Newbery Medal book you've read deserved the award, and why or why not.

Educator Notes

There are numerous websites which feature the Newbery Medal. Additional sites are listed below. In addition, many resources have been written on the Newbery Medal books which offer ways to implement the books into existing curriculum and educational standards.

Websites

Embracing The Child—Newbery Medal Booklist
> http://www.eyeontomorrow.com/embracingthechild/booknewlist.htm
> Author information and book reviews of medal-winning books.

History of the Newbery Medal
> http://www.widomaker.com/~ganderson/newhis.htm
> A good page which presents a history of the Newbery medal, selection criteria, and a description of the medal.

Newbery Award and Honor Books 1990s
> http://falcon.cfsd.k12.az.us/~ogwww/reviews/90newberys.html
> There are also selections from the 1980s, 1970s, and 1920s.

Newbery Medal

http://www.ucalgary.ca/~dkbrown/newbery.html

From the Children's Literature Web Guide, an excellent resource for information on children's literature. Contains numerous links, information, and resources.

The Newbery Medal

http://www.co.fairfax.va.us/library/reading/elem/newbery.htm

A site which lists the current medal winner and honor books for the John Newbery Medal. This web page is presented by the Fairfax County (VA) Library.

The Newbery Medal

http://ils.unc.edu/award/nhome.html

Good site with interesting information on the origin and selection of Newbery Medal books.

Newbery Medal and Honor Books

http://www.ucalgary.ca/~dkbrown/newb_hon.html

Complete list of Newbery Medal and Honor books presented by the Children's Literature Web Guide.

Newbery Medalists

http://awardbooks.hypermart.net/prod01.htm

Students can choose a Newbery Medal book and read a synopsis of the book. This site would be a good exploration of the Newbery books and may induce a desire to read additional titles.

Books

Comfort, Claudette Hegel. ***The Newbery and Caldecott Books in the Classroom.*** Incentive Publications, 1999. A handbook designed for classroom use, but adaptable to other educational settings.

Gillespie, John Thomas. ***The Newbery Companion: Booktalk and Related Materials for the Newbery Medal and Honor Books, 2nd Ed.*** Libraries Unlimited, 2001. Presents book talks for use in an educational setting.

Lewis, Marguerite Relyea. ***Hooked on the Newbery Award Winners: 75 Wordsearch Puzzles Based on the Newbery Gold Medal Books.*** Center for Applied Research, 1996. Includes crossword puzzles and wordsearch games.

Licciardo-Musso, Lori. ***Teaching with Favorite Newbery Books: Engaging Discussion Questions, Vocabulary Builders, Writing Prompts, and Great Literature Response Activities.*** Scholastic, 1999. Provides motivating activities that take students on literary journeys, and gives students an in-depth understanding of 25 Newbery books.

The Newbery and Caldecott Awards: A Guide to the Medal and Honor Books. American Library Association, 2001. Co-published by the Association for Library Service to Children.

Sarah, Plain and Tall
By Patricia MacLachlan
Harper, 1985 • Newbery Medal, 1986

Introduction

Sarah is from the East Coast. She is plain and tall, and moves to the Kansas prairie to be a mother and wife to a farm family. With her, Sarah brings stories of her life by the sea, and songs to share with her new family.

Assignment

As you read *Sarah, Plain and Tall*, think about stories from your own family. Each family has stories and tales which are a part of that family's history. It is interesting to know some of our stories because they can help us learn about our families and ourselves.

Internet Resources

Read *Sarah, Plain and Tall* or listen as your teacher reads it to your class. Think about Sarah and her new family. Think about the stories Sarah told of her life in the East near the ocean. Try to remember some family stories that your parents or grandparents have told you. If you were to interview an older family member, what are some questions you would ask? The Internet can help you develop questions and learn more about genealogy, or the study of family history.

Oral History Questions

    http://www.rootsweb.com/~genepool/oralhist.htm *Activities 1 & 2*

Roots Surname List – Interactive Search

    http://rsl.rootsweb.com/#search *Activities 3 & 4*

Draw a Coat of Arms

    http://ourworld.compuserve.com/homepages/Strawn/coatsofa.htm
    Activities 5 & 6

Activities

1. Who do you wish to interview?

2. Look at the questions in the Oral History Questions website. Use some of the ques-

tions to help you develop your own interview questions. List five questions you would ask in an oral history interview.

3. Look up your last name in the Roots Surname List. If your name does not appear, use the last name of a grandparent, aunt, uncle, cousin, or other relative.

4. What information did you learn about your surname?

5. See if you can find your surname or that of a friend on the Coat of Arms web page.

6. Explore some of the other coats of arms featured on this page.

7. Draw a coat of arms for your name using the information you learned.

Additional Activity

As part of your learning, complete the interview sheet that follows. This sheet can help you select a relative to interview about your family history. It will also help you think of questions to ask during the interview. After you interview a family member, share the information from your interview with the other class members. Does anyone have stories similar to yours? If available, you can include photographs of family members or other family treasures to share with your class.

Conclusion

As you read in *Sarah, Plain and Tall*, families are very important. Often our family will have stories which can be used to tell our history. During this lesson, we had the opportunity to learn about genealogy and oral history. As you get older, you may have the opportunity to share stories from when you were a child with your own children and help them learn!

Educator notes

There are numerous websites which discuss genealogy and oral history. Additional sites are listed below. In addition, many resources have been written which offer ways to implement storytelling into existing curriculum and educational standards.

Websites

Genealogical Journeys in Time

http://ourworld.compuserve.com/homepages/Strawn

A very good source for finding family information. Contains numerous links to additional information.

Genealogy Home Page

http://www.genhomepage.com

Provides good information and links on genealogy, including worldwide genealogy sources and mailing lists.

Patricia MacLachlan

http://www.randomhouse.com/teachers/authors/macl.html

Provides biographical information about Patricia MacLachlan and includes a message from Ms. MacLachlan.

Sarah, Plain and Tall

http://www.mce.k12tn.net/reading3/sarah.htm

A very nice site from an elementary school in Tennessee. On this page, students can work on vocabulary, activities, and questions pertaining to specific chapters in the book *Sarah, Plain and Tall*. An additional bonus are some Internet links for extra activities with the book.

Tips

http://ourworld.compuserve.com/homepages/Strawn/tips.htm

Includes research tips on gathering family information, a researcher's page with a form for recording information, and over 40,000 genealogy links.

Books

Beck, Jan C. ***Recording Words: Collecting Oral History and the Art of Interviewing.*** Vermont Folklife Center, 1994. A handbook on interviewing techniques, oral history, and background information on gathering oral histories.

Fletcher, William P. ***Recording Our Family History.*** Ten Speed, 1989. A guide to using video and audiotape to preserve family history. Also includes suggested topics, questions, and interview techniques.

Van Bommel, Harry. ***Your Personal Classic: Recording Your Life Story or Family History.*** PSD Consultants, 1994. Looking at autobiography as a literary form. Includes bibliographical references.

Our History is Oral

We all have a history. Some history is written, and some is presented as stories from our memories. They may be stories told to us by our parents or grandparents. Whatever the case, it is important to maintain these stories and add new ones. Through the use of an oral history interview, we can help the stories to come alive for the next generation. The Internet can help develop questions to use in an oral history interview.

Person you plan to interview

_____

Relationship to you

_____ _____

Date of interview _____

Place of interview_____

Birth date of person you plan to interview

_____

Topic or topics you wish to cover

_____

_____

_____

Method you plan to use to keep a record of the interview

_____

To help you develop questions for the interview, use the following Internet address:

Oral History Questions

http://www.rootsweb.com/~genepool/oralhist.htm

List ten questions that you plan to ask during your interview. Be sure to record the answers to your questions.

1. Question:

   Answer:

2. Question:

   Answer:

3. Question:

   Answer:

4. Question:

   Answer:

5. Question:

   Answer:

6. Question:

   Answer:

7. Question:

   Answer:

8. Question:

   Answer:

9. Question:

   Answer:

10. Question:

    Answer:

Summarize your interview, and be prepared to share with the class.

Roll of Thunder, Hear My Cry

By Mildred D. Taylor

Dial, 1976 • Newbery Medal, 1977

Introduction

Roll of Thunder, Hear My Cry is the story of the Logan family. Facing prejudice and discrimination in the South during the 1930s, the children in the Logan family struggle for understanding.

Assignment

Mildred D. Taylor's father was an accomplished storyteller. As she was growing up, Ms. Taylor was told stories and taught the history of her people through her father's stories. As you read *Roll of Thunder, Hear My Cry*, think of the stories that you have heard and told to others.

Internet Resources

After reading this book, begin your exploration of storytelling. Think of the history of storytelling, how it has affected your life, and ways you can continue the tradition. The Internet can help you learn about storytelling, learn how to tell a story, and find stories to tell to an audience.

Storytelling, Definition and Purpose

http://www.peg.apc.org/~dbelling/WhatIsStlg.html *Activities 1 & 2*

The Art of the Storyteller

http://www.seanet.com/~eldrbarry/roos/storytel.htm *Activity 3*

Storytelling Described by Chuck Larkin

http://www.seanet.com/~eldrbarry/roos/st_is.htm *Activity 4*

Tips on Selection and Learning Stories

http://www.cinenet.net/users/mhnadel/story/tips.html *Activities 5 & 6*

Telling Your Story

http://www.aaronshep.com/storytelling/Tips3.html *Activity 7*

Activities

1. What is a definition of storytelling?

2. What are three reasons to tell stories?

3. Royalty often hired storytellers to tell tales of court or heroic accomplishments. What were these storytellers called?

4. What are two types of storytellers?

5. When choosing a story, what are four things which you need in your story?

6. As you learn a story, writing six important facts on a card can help you with the story. What are those six things?

7. A good place for storytelling is _____, _____, and _____.

Additional Activity

You have learned about storytelling and read tips on how to tell a story, and now it is time to select a story to tell to your class. Choose a story from a book or from one of the Internet sites below. After you have practiced your story and feel comfortable, share your story with other students who have been studying the art of storytelling.

Online Children's Stories

http://www.acs.ucalgary.ca/~dkbrown/stories.html
Story collections, folklore, poetry, and classics for young children. From the Children's Literature Web Guide, an excellent source for the study and enjoyment of children's literature.

Storyteller.net

http://www.storyteller.net
Listen to the "Story of the Week," stories from selected storytellers, or visit the playground, which has online games that feature storytelling.

Storytelling Library: Aesop's ABC

http://www.storyarts.org/library/aesops/index.html
This web page features an Aesop's Fable for each letter of the alphabet. By choosing a fable, children are directed to another page where they can read their selection.

Conclusion

As you read in *Roll of Thunder, Hear My Cry*, stories can offer us history, excitement and knowledge. Everyone has a story to tell, and everyone is a storyteller. Practicing the stories you learn allows you to continue the tradition of the oral story.

Educator Notes

There are many websites which are devoted to the Newbery Medal book *Roll of Thunder, Hear My Cry*, as well as Mildred D. Taylor, the author. If you wish to further extend this activity, explore these websites with the children.

Websites

Mildred D. Taylor

http://www.randomhouse.com/teachers/authors/tayl.html

Interview with Mildred D. Taylor and excerpt from a speech by Ms. Taylor, presented by Random House.

Mildred Taylor

http://falcon.jmu.edu/~ramseyil/taylor.htm

Background information on Mildred D. Taylor, lesson plans for *Roll of Thunder, Hear My Cry,* and a bibliography of Taylor's works. A good educational resource.

The Novels of Mildred D. Taylor

http://www.randomhouse.com/teachers/authors/nomt.html

Provides an overview of some of Ms. Taylor's novels, background information on the novels, and teaching ideas for using the novels in an educational setting.

Roll of Thunder Hear My Cry

http://www.ced.appstate.edu/whs/rollthun.htm

Analysis and children's reviews of the Newbery Medal book.

Mildred D. Taylor Teacher Resource File

http://falcon.jmu.edu/~ramseyil/taylor.htm

Part of the Internet School Library Media Page, this web page features lesson plans, book reviews, a biography and other resources for use with books authored by Mildred D. Taylor. An excellent resource for teachers, school librarians, and parents, this page offers much information for use in the classroom.

Books

Dubrovin, Vivian. ***Create Your Own Storytelling Stories.*** Storycraft, 1995. Explains the art of storytelling for children.

Kindig, Eileen S. ***Remember the Time ...? The Power & Promise of Family Storytelling.*** InterVarsity Press, 1997. This book is designed to help create stronger environments for family stories and storytelling.

Naegelin, Lanny. ***Getting Started in Oral Interpretation.*** NTC Contemporary, 1995. Instruction for children on oral interpretation and storytelling. A good resource for the classroom, home or library.

Pellowski, Anne. ***The Storytelling Handbook: A Young People's Collection of Unusual Tales & Helpful Hints on How to Tell Them.*** Simon & Schuster, 1995. Anne Pellowski is well-known for her books on storytelling, and this volume is another excellent resource.

Julie of the Wolves

By Jean Craighead George

Harper, 1972 • Newbery Medal, 1973

Introduction

Julie was abandoned in the Alaskan wilderness. As she watched the wolves while sitting at her camp, Julie realized she would need the wolves to help her survive. When Julie learns the language of the wolves, she is accepted by them.

Assignment

After reading *Julie of the Wolves,* think about what it would be like to live as one of the wolves from this story—hunting for food each day, living in the cold Alaskan wilderness, and facing the need for survival.

Internet Resources

Wolf

> http://encarta.msn.com/find/Concise.asp?z=1&pg=2&ti=761560395 *Activities 1 & 2*

Learn About Wolves

> http://www.wolf.org/visit/visitfrm.htm *Activities 3 & 4 & 5*

White Wolf Sounds

> http://www.sonic.net/~rodney1/sounds.htm *Activity 6*
> (Requires necessary computer equipment)

Activities

1. What two animals is a wolf related to?

2. What are the two species of wolves?

3. How much does the average female wolf from Minnesota weigh? How much does an average male wolf weigh? What do we know about the largest wolf from Alaska?

4. According to 1997–98 estimates, how many wolves were there in Minnesota?

5. What is the average number of wolf pups born in a litter?

6. Which wolf howl is your favorite? Why?

Additional Activity

Wolves are creatures of the wild. Much is being done to preserve the wolf packs and their habitat. Education is the key to understanding the wolf and its needs. Share with your class ways that you would work to help save the wolf. What type of educational programs would you develop? Would you allow people to "adopt" wolves, and what would you do to help wolf conservation? Share your ideas with your class through a report or visual presentation.

Conclusion

As you read in *Julie of the Wolves*, the wolf is an interesting and intelligent animal. It is necessary to respect wolves and to educate others about wolves and their environment. Through conservation and knowledge about wolves, we can learn to understand and value the role that the wolf plays in our world.

Educator Notes

The following websites feature additional information about wolves and their environment. Some of the sites include multiple links and educational activities. In addition, the author of *Julie of the Wolves*, Jean Craighead George, is featured on the World Wide Web.

Websites

International Wolf Center

http://www.wolf.org/visit/visitfrm.htm

Educational programs and resources with "Wolves and Humans" teacher's guide.

Jean Craighead George

http://www.jeancraigheadgeorge.com/

The home page of Jean Craighead George with brief information on other books she has written.

Jean Craighead George

http://www.harpercollins.com/authors/pages/George_Jean-Craighead.htm

Biographical information about Jean Craighead George, presented by HarperCollins.

National Parks Conservation Association

http://www.npca.org/wildlife_protection/wildlife_facts/wolf.asp

Provides facts, pictures and statistics on wolves in America. This page would be useful when studying the need to protect the wild wolves in our country.

Superior National Forest Wolf Telemetry Data

http://www.wolf.org/telemsearch/telemsearch.phtml

Provides access to telemetry data about wolves. (Requires standard database software)

Wolf Haven International

http://www.wolfhaven.org/

Contains numerous links which provide information about wolves from fact sheets to information about the wolf adoption program.

Books

Dudley, Karen. **Wolves.** Raintree Steck-Vaughn, 1997. Part of the Untamed World series. This book would make a good curriculum extension.

George, Jean Craighead. **Look to the North: A Wolf Pup Diary.** HarperCollins, 1997. Another story about wolves by the author of *Julie of the Wolves*. This book is suitable for younger children.

Gobel, Paul. **Dream Wolf.** Simon & Schuster, 1997. A look at wolves by the Caldecott Award winning author.

Smith, Roland. **Journey of the Red Wolf.** Dutton, 1996. A look at wildlife conservation for grades 5–8.

A Gathering of Days
A New England Girl's Journal, 1830-1832

By Joan W. Blos

Scribner, 1979 • Newbery Medal, 1980

Introduction

Catherine is thirteen years old when she begins her journal. In this story, we meet Catherine, her family, and her friends. *A Gathering of Days* is a story of life told through the eyes of a young girl.

Assignment

Writing in a journal is a good way to record thoughts, feelings, and the events in our lives. Keeping a journal allows us to review our lives and share our history with others. It is also fun to read our journals after we have grown.

Internet Resources

After reading *A Gathering of Days*, it might be fun to begin a journal. But first, you will need to learn some important aspects of journal keeping. By using the Internet, you can learn about journals and find hints on keeping a journal.

What Is a Journal?

http://www.nzdances.co.nz/journal/whatis.htm *Activity 1*

How Do I Write a Journal?

http://www.nzdances.co.nz/journal/howto.htm *Activity 2*

The Goals of the Journal Writer?

http://www.nzdances.co.nz/journal/goals.htm *Activity 3*

What Benefits Will I Get?

http://www.nzdances.co.nz/journal/benefits.htm *Activity 4*

Writing a Diary As a Journal

http://www.nzdances.co.nz/journal/diary.htm *Activity 5*

Anne's Legacy

http://www.annefrank.nl/eng/diary/textdagboek/textDB3_3.html *Activity 6*

Activities

1. What is a journal? What are some types of journals?

2. What are the four main methods of journal writing? Give a brief explanation of each.

3. What are nine suggested specific objectives of a journal?

4. What is the best reason for keeping a journal?

5. The most common method of writing a journal is to...?

6. One of the most famous journals is *The Diary of Anne Frank*. What was the original title of the book and when was it first published?

Additional Activity

After completing your study of journals, continue to write in your journal. Write about topics that interest you, thoughts you have about school or friends. As you continue to keep your journal, you may find interesting aspects of your life which you did not realize to be true.

Conclusion

Keep your journals in a safe place. At the end of the year, read what you have written. Are you surprised by your words and thoughts? When you are an adult, reread your journals. Do you think you will remember the events you wrote about? Will you have similar thoughts? Journals are a good way to record our history and to share with others.

Educator Notes

The following websites and resource books provide additional information about journals, diaries and journal writing for children.

Websites

The Story of the Diary

http://www.annefrank.com/site/af_student/study_STORY.htm
A useful study guide about The Diary of Anne Frank, the information presented on this web page would benefit a unit on the Diary or Anne Frank.

Indexing Your Journal

http://www.nzdances.co.nz/journal/indexing.htm

For advanced journal writers who have been keeping a journal for some time.

A Journal and Family Issues

http://www.nzdances.co.nz/journal/family.htm

Using a journal to help understand the family. This page is geared toward adults, but can be adapted for classroom use.

National Journal Network

http://www.geocities.com/SoHo/9993/

The page of a group of journal writers, with ideas for writing.

Journal Writing with Virginia Hamilton

http://teacher.scholastic.com/writewit/diary/tguide.htm

Includes a 14-day free trial of Scholastic Network. One of the highlights is "Writing with Writers: Diary writing with Virginia Hamilton."

Why Write a Journal?

http://www.nzdances.co.nz/journal/whywrite.htm

For those wondering why people keep journals.

Books

Albert, Susan W. *Writing From Life: Telling Your Soul's Story.* Putnam, 1997. Autobiographical writing, geared toward adults, but with some helpful ideas which can be adapted for classroom use.

Green, Donna. *Anne of Green Gables Journal.* Vermillion, 1997. A calendar/journal book for juveniles, based on *Anne of Green Gables,* a classic for young adults.

Pages & Pockets: A Portfolio for Secrets & Stuff. Pleasant Co., 1995. From the publishers of the American Girls series. History presented in a way children enjoy.

Zimmerman, William. *A Book of Questions to Keep Thoughts & Feelings.* Guarionex, 1994. Questions to aid in the process of writing a journal that is useful with children.

Joyful Noise
Poems for Two Voices
By Paul Fleischman
Harper, 1988 • Newbery Medal, 1989

Introduction

Poetry can be compared to songs, words, thoughts and feelings. In *Joyful Noise,* Paul Fleischman has collected poems which can be read by two people, and enjoyed by all.

Assignment

As you read *Joyful Noise* with a partner, begin to think of poems that you have enjoyed. Also, start to think about poems that you can write. What would you like to write a poem about? Do you know about different types of poems? Poems are more than just words, they are expression.

Internet Resources

The Academy of American Poets—National Poetry Month

    http://www.poets.org/npm/npmmain.htm   *Activity 1*

Poetry Writing Tips

    http://www.azstarnet.com/~poewar/writer/Poet's_Notes.html   *Activities 2, 3 & 4*

Ask Earl—Poetry

    http://www.yahooligans.com/content/ask_earl/20011012.html   *Activities 5 & 6*

Activities

1. When is National Poetry Month? What is the purpose of National Poetry Month?

2. If you have problems writing a poem, what does the author suggest you do?

3. Where are some places you can write for help?

4. When trying to write, what should you do for one minute to help you write when

experiencing "writer's block?"

5. What are three types of poetry?

6. Write your own cinquain poem.

Additional Activity

Share your cinquain (Activity 6) with your class and then try writing a diamante poem or a limerick. Use the following site to find your information:

Notes for Using Poetry with Children

http://weber.u.washington.edu/~belinda/class/poetry.html

Conclusion

Poetry is a variety of words, thoughts and expressions. Not all poems need to rhyme. Everyone has their own distinct style of writing poetry. During this lesson, we had the opportunity to learn tips to writing poetry and try our hand at writing our own poems.

Educator Notes

The following selected list of print and electronic resources is intended for use by teachers to aid in the instruction process.

Websites

The Academy of American Poets – Educator Tips

http://www.poets.org/npm/teachtip.htm

Numerous suggestions for incorporating poetry into the classroom, including preparation, writing, reading and other activities.

I Live on a Raft

http://collection.nlc-bnc.ca/100/200/300/concertina/raft/rafttoc.htm

Online poems to share with children.

KidzPage! Poetry and Verse for Children of All Ages

http://web.aimnet.com/~veeceet/kids/kidzpage.html

Poetry written by children, for children with numerous topics and links.

The Poetry Zone

http://www.poetryzone.ndirect.co.uk/index2.htm

A fun place to visit that features poetry for and by children, links to poets and a teacher zone that offers suggestions for the use of poetry in the classroom.

Scholastic's Writing with Writers—Poetry

http://teacher.scholastic.com/writewit/poetry/index.htm

A series of poetry writing lessons, plus writing tips from Jack Prelutsky. Available with an account from Scholastic Network.

StoryTellers Challenge Poem

http://www.ribscage.com/STPoems/stpmlist.asp

Collaborative poetry writing with submission forms.

Word Dance—Sharing Poetry With Children

http://www.washingtonparent.com/articles/9709/poetry.htm

Provides useful information on sharing poetry with children. Written for parents, this information can be used in the classroom as well.

Books

Bumgardner, Joyce C. *Helping Students Learn to Write Poetry: An Idea Book for Poets of All Ages.* Allyn & Bacon, 1996. Designed for use in language arts, English and creative writing classes.

Dias, Patrick. *Reading & Responding to Poetry: Patterns in the Process.* Boynton Cook, 1995. Useful for language arts, literature, literary criticism, and the teaching of poetry.

Leggo, Carol. *Teaching to Wonder: Responding to Wonder in the Secondary Classroom.* Orca, 1997. Information on the study and teaching of poetry and use in the classroom.

Perry, Aaren Y. *Poetry Across the Curriculum: An Action Guide for Elementary Teachers.* Ally & Bacon, 1996. Although designed for elementary teachers, some of the ideas are adaptable for older students.

Sedgwick, Fred. *Read My Mind: Young Children, Poetry & Learning.* Routledge, 1997. The study, teaching, and authorship of poetry with young children.

LQ7

Lincoln
A Photobiography
By Russell Freedman
Clarion, 1987 • Newbery Medal, 1988

Introduction

Lincoln: A Photobiography is a biographical story of Abraham Lincoln, our nation's sixteenth President. This story is told with numerous photographs of Abraham Lincoln and our country during his lifetime.

Assignment

Abraham Lincoln is one of our most famous Presidents. His work to end slavery and reunite the United States was very important. As you read *Lincoln: A Photobiography*, think about how our sixteenth President changed the history of the U. S.

Internet Resources

The following Internet sources can help you in your exploration of Abraham Lincoln's life.

The History Place

   http://www.historyplace.com/lincoln/index.html   *Activities 1, 2 & 3*

The American Presidency

   http://gi.grolier.com/presidents/aae/quickfac/16flinc.html   *Activity 4*

Abraham Lincoln

   http://www.whitehouse.gov/history/presidents/al16.html   *Activity 5*

Activities

1. When was Abraham Lincoln born? Where was he born?

2. Which political party did Abraham Lincoln help organize in 1856? What happened at the first convention of this party?

3. When was Abraham Lincoln elected president? How many electoral votes did he receive?

4. What were Abraham Lincoln's nicknames?

5. What were Lincoln's thoughts on secession of the Southern states? When did Lincoln ask for volunteers to fight in the Civil War?

Additional Activity

Share with your classmates the information that you have gained during this assignment. Perhaps you can make a timeline of important dates in the life of Abraham Lincoln. Be sure to include his birth, marriage, election to the Presidency, and death. Highlight the important events of Lincoln's presidency.

Conclusion

Abraham Lincoln was one of our great American leaders. He envisioned an unified America and helped direct the Civil War which brought about the end of slavery. Abraham Lincoln rose from a simple life to become the most powerful man in America. By reading *Lincoln: A Photobiography* you had the opportunity to read about his life and to view photographs of him, his family, and the United States during the Civil War.

Educator Notes

Numerous websites provide information about Abraham Lincoln, the Civil War, and slavery. A few sites, which have been chosen for their educational value are listed below. In addition, the list includes a selection of the many books that have been published on these topics.

Websites

Abraham Lincoln

http://www.uky.edu/Biography/lincoln-abraham.html

Short biographical information about Abraham Lincoln with links to sites in Kentucky of importance in Lincoln's life.

Abraham Lincoln

http://www1.whitehouse.gov/WH/glimpse/presidents/html/al16.html

Extensive site with facts, biographical information, and quotes from Abraham Lincoln.

Abraham Lincoln for Primary Children

http://www.siec.k12.in.us/~west/proj/lincoln/

Web-based activities including an online quiz and picture gallery. Designed for primary children, but contains activities and information appropriate for adaptation.

Abraham Lincoln Online

http://www.netins.net/showcase/creative/lincoln.html

Numerous links and resources for the study of Abraham Lincoln. A good starting point for Lincoln research.

Abraham Lincoln's Assassination

http://members.aol.com/RVSNorton/Lincoln.html

An Internet site devoted to the assassination of Abraham Lincoln. Additional links include books, photographs, and information on John Wilkes Booth.

Lincoln Memorial Homepage

http://www.nps.gov/linc/

Information about the Lincoln Memorial in Washington DC. Includes a description and photograph of the Memorial.

New Book of Knowledge: Abraham Lincoln

http://gi.grolier.com/presidents/nbk/bios/16plinc.html

Extensive site on Abraham Lincoln from Grolier Online with Quick Facts on Lincoln and text of his Inaugural Addresses from 1861 and 1865.

Books

Bracken, Thomas. ***Abraham & Mary Lincoln.*** Chelsea House, 1997. An informative look at Abraham Lincoln and his wife, Mary Todd Lincoln.

Uglow, Lloyd. ***Abraham Lincoln, Will You Ever Give Up?*** Advance Publishing, 1996. Part of the Great Achiever series, this book focuses on Abraham Lincoln.

MacDonald, Fiona. ***The World in the Time of Abraham Lincoln.*** Silver Burdett, 1997. Features Abraham Lincoln and the world during the nineteenth century.

Weinberg, Larry. ***Abraham Lincoln: President for the People.*** Gareth Stevens, 1997. A look at the sixteenth president of the United States for grades 3 and up.

Number the Stars

By Lois Lowry

Houghton Mifflin, 1989 • Newbery Medal, 1990

Introduction

Number the Stars is a moving story about the Johansen and Rosen families during World War II. The Rosens are Jewish, and they fear for their lives. Their friends, the Johansen family, decide to jeopardize their own lives to help the Rosens during this time of terror.

Assignment

As you read this story, try to imagine what it would be like to have your life threatened because of your religion. Try to imagine what it would be like to have your life change because of who you are and what you believe in. Think of the millions of people who lost their lives during the Holocaust.

Internet Resources

The Holocaust was a time of great strife and heartbreak in the history of our world. Much has been written about the Holocaust and its repercussions. The Internet has many resources available about the Holocaust, a few of which are represented by the resources listed below.

Five Questions About the Holocaust

    http://www.geocities.com/Paris/5121/5questions.htm *Activities 1 & 2*

36 Questions About the Holocaust

    http://motlc.wiesenthal.com/resources/questions/index.html *Activities 3 & 4*

Anne Frank's Life and Times: The Diary

    http://www.annefrank.com/site/af_life/2_life_exrpt/2_life_diary.htm *Activity 5*

Children of the Holocaust

    http://www.graceproducts.com/fmnc/main.htm *Activity 6*

Activities

1. What was the Holocaust? When did it happen? Who were the primary targets of the Holocaust?

2. What did the German Nazis believe?

3. How many Jewish people were killed during the Holocaust?

4. What does the term "death camp" mean? How many death camps were there during the Holocaust, and where were they located?

5. One of the most well-known Holocaust stories is that of Anne Frank. When did Anne and her family go into hiding from the Nazis? Pick a date from the *Diary* and read what Anne wrote. Record your thoughts upon reading her entry. Do you find sadness? Hope? Joy? Fear? Do you believe you can understand what Anne was feeling? Why or why not?

6. Pick the name of one child from "Children of the Holocaust." Read the information presented about this child. What did you find out about the child?

Additional Activity

The Holocaust is a difficult time period to understand. It is hard for us to imagine why people were killed. As part of your learning, share your thoughts and feelings with the class. How would you feel if your family had been part of the Holocaust? How would it feel to fear for your life? Would you like to spend days, months, or years in hiding? It is important to always strive for peace among the people of the world. Use your learning to develop ways to ensure peace in our world so that the Holocaust does not repeat itself. Share your ideas with the class.

Conclusion

As we study the Holocaust, perhaps we can learn about ourselves and how we can make our world a better place to live. It is important to respect human life and the beliefs of others. *Number the Stars* is a good book, which teaches a valuable lesson. You may wish to find an adult with whom to share this book and discuss your feelings about the Holocaust.

Educator notes

The following sites are a few of the ones which are available about the Holocaust. Also included are some sites about the author of *Number the Stars*, Lois Lowry, and resource books for use in the classroom.

LearningQuest 8 : number the Stars

Websites

Anne Frank Bookscape

http://www.ctnba.org/ctn/k8/anne.html

Includes links for lesson plans, Holocaust resources on the Internet, discussion sites, and survivor memories.

Children and the Holocaust

http://www.ushmm.org/wlc/article.jsp?ModuleId=10005142

Provides information, statistics, and background on the children of the Holocaust.

Guidelines for Teaching About the Holocaust

http://www.ushmm.org/education/foreducators/teachabo/right.htm

Designed for educators teaching about the Holocaust and related subjects. Provides a list of considerations for incorporating a Holocaust study into existing classes.

Holocaust Books for Children

http://www.holocaust-trc.org/chldbook.htm

Annotated book reviews for children who wish to read more about the Holocaust. Includes fiction and nonfiction works.

Holocaust Memorial Center Links

http://holocaustcenter.org/links/links_ghr.shtml

Lists numerous links about the Holocaust, including Anne Frank Online, The Simon Wiesenthal Center, and the United States Holocaust Memorial Museum

IPL Youth Division: Ask the Author

http://www.ipl.org/youth/AskAuthor/Lowry.html

An article written by Lois Lowry. In the article, she provides answers to questions about her life, writing, and goals.

Learning About Lois Lowry

http://www.scils.rutgers.edu/special/kay/lowry.html

Includes a biography, information about her novels, bibliography, and book reviews.

Lois Lowry

www.randomhouse.com/teachers/authors/lowr.html

Includes facts about Lois Lowry, a message from the author, and links to a few of her books.

Number the Stars

http://www.ncsa.uiuc.edu/edu/Affiliates/Elgin/NUMBER/nsdoc.htm

Provides author information, book reviews, and information about World War II.

Number the Stars by Lois Lowry

http://www.carolhurst.com/titles/numberthestars.html

Educational activities, book reviews, and related literature to supplement an instructional unit on *Number the Stars.*

Writing for Children

http://www.mps.k12.vt.us/ues/lowry.html

This is an article written by Lois Lowry on how she became a writer for children. This site should interest her fans, as well as those interested in the craft of writing.

Books

Brooks, Philip. *The United States Holocaust Memorial Museum.* Children's Press, 1997. Presents information about the United States Holocaust Memorial Museum for children.

Elli's Tales Growing Up in the Holocaust. Simon & Schuster, 1997. A child's view of the Holocaust.

Epstein, Rachel S. *Anne Frank.* Franklin Watts, 1997. A look at Anne Frank for young children.

Gold, Alison L. *No Time for Good-Bye: Memories of Anne Frank.* Scholastic, 1997. A biographical account of Anne Frank.

Lace, William W. *The Death Camps.* Lucent, 1997. This title covers the death camps and their relationship to the war. Part of The Holocaust Library series.

Sherrow, Victoria. *The Blaze Engulfs: January 1939 to December 1941.* Blackbirch, 1997. Provides background information on the Jews in Germany and the Holocaust.

Rice, Earle. *The Final Solution.* Lucent, 1997. A look at the Holocaust years, 1939–1945.

The View from Saturday

By E. L. Konigsburg

Jean Karl/Atheneum, 1996 • Newbery Medal, 1997

Introduction

The four members of the Academic Bowl team become fast friends in this story by two-time Newbery Award-winner E. L. Konigsburg. The story is told from the point of view of each character, and through the story we learn about the children, their hopes, their dreams, and their interwoven lives.

Assignment

As you read *The View from Saturday,* think about the friends that you have. Are there new friends, friends you've had for a long time, or is there someone else you wish you were friends with? Think of what it means to be a friend, and how you can be a friend to others.

Internet Resources

The Definition of Friendship
    http://dictionary.msn.com/ *Activity 1*

The Friendship Dolls
    http://www.clas.ufl.edu/users/jshoaf/Jdolls/friendship.htm *Activity 2*

JADE Enduring Friendships
    http://www.jadejapandolls.com/friend1.htm *Activity 3*

Miss Fujiko Yamanashi Friendship Doll Collection
    http://spacr.state.wy.us/cr/wsm/yampg1.htm *Activity 4*

Kids.Com Keypal
    http://www.kidscom.com/cgi-bin/keypal/keypal_search.pl *Activity 5*

Enter Keypals Club International
> http://www.worldkids.net/clubs/kci/keypals2.html *Activity 6*

Activities

1. According to the *Encarta Dictionary*, what is the definition of the word "friend?" What is *your* definition of the word "friend?"

2. What were the Friendship Dolls? How many dolls were sent from Japan to the United States?

3. Who provided the inspiration for the dolls?

4. What is "Hina Matsuri?"

5. The role of the computer has changed our idea of penpals. In order to be a proper "keypal," it is necessary to follow certain rules. What are four suggestions to help people be proper keypals?

6. With the assistance of your teacher, follow the steps to become a "keypal." Report to the class on your success and what your wrote in you keypal message.

Additional Activity

As you establish regular communication with your keypal, update the members of your class on your experiences. Having a keypal provides you the opportunity to converse with someone in another part of the country or world. You may also have the opportunity to learn new customs, language and information about your keypal and their world.

Conclusion

Friendship is a special relationship between people. There are many types of friends, and being a friend is important to others. There are many ways to express friendship, such as keypals and the Friendship Dolls. Think of ways that you can continue to be a friend to people in our world.

Educator Notes

Additional sites and books focus on friendships made in the classroom and through keypal connections.

Websites

ALSC: The John Newbery Medal
> http://www.ala.org/alsc/n1997.html
> Features information on *The View from Saturday.*

Education Center Activity: Friendship Gallery

http://www.eduplace.com/act/gallery.html

An activity which encourages children to share their ideas of friendship with classmates.

Education Center Activity: Friendship Mobiles

http://www.eduplace.com/act/mobiles.html

A science and art activity which discusses elements of nature and how these elements can be our "friends."

Give Children Friendship Tips

http://www.cyfc.umn.edu/Parenting/Familylife/friendshiptips.html

A "Family Life Packet" that gives tips on how children can make and keep friends.

Keypals Connect Students Around the World

http://www.learningspace.org/ric/gprojects/ricglobal.html

Provides information for teachers on managing keypals, finding keypals and links to various keypal sites on the Internet.

Parents: Helping Children make Friends

http://linden.fortnet.org/ParentToParent/PFellers/par_frnd.html

Provides information on fostering friendship among children. Contains good tips which can be adapted for any educational setting.

The View from Saturday

http://www.uwstout.edu/lib/ch/bookdesc.htm

A description of the book is provided on this web page. Educators can use this page as an introduction to the book, plus find additional information in the provided bibliography.

Books

Deegan, James C. ***Children's Friendships in Culturally Diverse Classrooms.*** Taylor & Francis, 1996. Encouraging friendships between children of diverse cultures in multiethnic situations.

Frankel, Fred. ***Good Friends Are Hard to Find Help Your Child Find, Make & Keep Friends.*** Perspective, 1996. Discussion of friendship and social skills for children. Designed for parents, but with educational applications.

McCoy, Sharon. ***50 Nifty Super Friendship Crafts.*** Lowell House, 1997. Crafts which friends can make and give to each other.

Schmidt, John J. ***Making & Keeping Friends: Rady-to-Use Lessons, Stories & Activities for Building Relationships.*** Center for Applied Research, 1997. Activity programs for fostering friendships between children. Designed for educational settings.

From the Mixed-Up Files of Mrs. Basil E. Frankweiler

By E. L. Konigsburg

Atheneum, 1967 • Newbery Medal, 1968

Introduction

Claudia Kincaid and her brother Jamie decide to run away and live at the Metropolitan Museum of Art in New York City. While there, they discover a statue of an angel and go looking for the former owner of the statue, Mrs. Basil E. Frankweiler.

Assignment

As you read *From the Mixed-Up Files of Mrs. Basil E. Frankweiler,* think about a museum you have visited, or would like to visit. Many museums have paintings, sculpture, or other works of art. The Internet can help you explore different types of art and gain an appreciation for the artists. Use the following sites to expand your knowledge about art museums.

Welcome to The Metropolitan Museum of Art

http://www.metmuseum.org *Activity 1*

Art Game

http://www.metmuseum.org/explore/FUN/artgame1.html *Activity 2*

What Does a Curator Do?

http://www.metmuseum.org/explore/FAQ/htm/curator.htm *Activity 3*

Symbols

http://www.metmuseum.org/explore/symbols/html/el_symbols_fm.htm *Activity 4*

The Metropolitan Museum of Art News

http://www.metmuseum.org/news/index.htm *Activity 5*

Smithsonian Institution Times

http://www.150.si.edu/smithexb/sitime.htm *Activity 6*

Activities

1. Where is the Metropolitan Museum of Art located? How many works of art are housed in the museum's collections?

2. Choose two "details" to explore. What did you see? Look at the detail of the larger image. Is it cloth, hair, or a tree?

3. What does the word curator mean? What is one thing a curator at the Metropolitan Museum of art does?

4. Click one of the images to explore symbols in art. What does the symbol mean? Did you like the artwork you looked at? Why or why not?

5. Choose one of the links in "What's New in the Galleries." Write a short report on your findings, and illustrate your report with a drawing of something you saw.

6. Another famous American museum is the Smithsonian Museum in Washington, D.C. In what year was the Smithsonian Act of Organization signed into law? Who was President of the United States? Choose five different years in the history of the Smithsonian and present an important fact from each of those years.

Additional Activity

Learning about museums is very much a visual experience. Often a trip to the museum is in looking and experiencing art through sight. Choose a picture you saw in your exploration of The Metropolitan Museum of Art or The Smithsonian and draw it for your classmates. After you have completed your picture, share it with your class and tell the class a bit about the picture. Who was the original artist? What medium did the artist use to complete the picture? When was it completed?

Conclusion

As you read in *From the Mixed-Up Files of Mrs. Basil E. Frankweiler,* an art museum is a place of many events and things to see. Through the Internet we have the opportunity to visit museums around the world through the use of our computers. We can gain an appreciation for art and the artists who produce famous works.

Educator Notes

Continue your cyberstudy of museums and art galleries with the websites and books in this section. There are also numerous resources for extending the classroom study of E. L. Konigsburg's stories and *The Mixed-Up Files* in particular.

Websites

ALSC: About E. L. Konigsburg

http://www.ala.org/alsc/konigs.html

Facts about the author, awards she has won, and a bibliography of Konigsburg created by the Association of Library Service to Children.

Teachers@Random—E. L. Konigsburg

http://www.randomhouse.com/teachers/authors/koni.html

Facts about the author of *From the Mixed-Up Files of Mrs. Basil E. Frankweiler.*

Teachers@Random—*From the Mixed-Up Files of Mrs. Basil E. Frankweiler*

http://www.randomhouse.com/teachers/authors/basi.html

A teacher's guide featuring information about the book, an excerpt, thematic connections, and related titles.

Collection Tours

http://www.metmuseum.org/collections/index.asp

Summaries of recent exhibitions at the Metropolitan Museum of Art in New York.

Bookscape: From the Mixed-Up Files of Mrs. Basil E. Frankweiler

http://www.ctnba.org/ctn/k8/mixedup.html

A bookscape on the book, featuring maps of New York City, The Metropolitan Museum of Art Homepage, links to art and artists, and discussion questions.

Metropolitan Museum of Art Special Exhibitions

http://www.metmuseum.org/special/index.asp

Close up view of current exhibitions at the museum.

Hands On Children's Museum on the Web

http://www.hocm.org/

Extensive site with links to children's museums as well as other links to other sites for children.

The Mona Lisa

http://www.paris.org/Musees/Louvre/Treasures/gifs/Mona_Lisa.jpg

Nice image of the Mona Lisa, which hangs in the Louvre.

PIGS Space: Novel Studies - From the Mixed-Up Files of Mrs. Basil E. Frankweiler

http://cspace.unb.ca/nbco/pigs/novel/social2.html

Questions about the *Mixed-Up Files* that focus on the social dilemmas faced by children.

PIGS Space: Novel Studies - From the Mixed-Up Files of Mrs. Basil E. Frankweiler

http://cspace.unb.ca/nbco/pigs/novel/active2.html

Cooperative activities based on the *Mixed-Up Files* for children in grades 4–8.

SCORE Teacher Guide: From the Mixed-Up Files of Mrs. Basil E. Frankweiler
> http://www.sdcoe.k12.ca.us/score/fris/fristg.htm
> A CyberGuide, similar to a LearningQuest, in which children examine the elements of art.

A Tour of the Louvre
> http://www.smartweb.fr/louvre/globale.htm
> Presents a selective tour and history of the Louvre in Paris, France.

Books

American Treasures. Reader's Digest, 1997. Includes information on American museums and national parks.

Burn, Barbara. ***Masterpieces from the Metropolitan Museum of Art.*** Metropolitan Museum of Art, 1997. Exhibitions and art from the Metropolitan collections.

Kallen, Stuart and Berg, Julie. ***The Museum.*** Abdo & Daughters, 1997. A Field Trips series book featuring children's museums.

Knopf Guide to the Louvre. Translated by Susan Mackervoy, Anthony Roberts and Simon Dalgleish. Knopf, 1995. A children's guide to the Louvre, including information on the appreciation of fine art.

Thomson, Peggy. ***The Nine-Ton Cat and Other True Tales of an Art Museum.*** Houghton Mifflin, 1997. Information from the National Gallery of Art. This is a good factual representation for use with children.

Maniac Magee

By Jerry Spinelli
Little Brown, 1990 • Newbery Medal, 1991

Introduction

Jeffrey Lionel Magee, better known as Maniac Magee, was on the run. He ended up in the town of Two Mills and there he became a legend. He was not only a legend for his running, baseball, and skills with a knot, but because of his ability to bring strangers together.

Assignment

Maniac Magee is more than a story about a boy and his athletic ability. *Maniac Magee* is a story which will cause you to think and examine your own life. As you read this story, think about sports and the role they play in your life. Also think about how you can make the world a better place in which to live.

Internet Resources

Children & Sports

> http://www.aacap.org/publications/factsfam/sports.htm *Activities 1 & 2*

Yahooligans! Sports Page

> http://www.yahooligans.com/content/spa *Activity 3*

Finding a Sport for Your Child

> http://www.vh.org/Patients/IHB/Peds/General/Sports.html *Activity 4*

Sports Injuries

> http://www.nih.gov/news/WordonHealth/jun2000/story07.htm *Activities 5 & 6*

Activities

1. What are seven things that sports help children do?

2. What are three ways parents and adults can help children get the most from sports?

3. Pick your favorite sport from the list provided. What is the latest news in your favorite sport? What are the standings of teams in the sport?

4. What are five ways in which sports differ?

5. What are three ways to prevent sports injury?

6. What does the acronym RICE stand for? When would you use RICE?

Additional Activity

As part of your learning, research the ancient Olympics using the following URL:

http://www.perseus.tufts.edu/Olympics/

Answer the question, "Where did the Olympic games come from?" Report your findings to your class.

Conclusion

As you read in *Maniac Magee*, sports have a way of bringing people together. Whether on the playing field, the coaching staff, or in the stands, sports allow people with a common interest to spend time together enjoying a favorite pastime.

Educator Notes

The websites in this section include several that are extensions of *Maniac Magee* and directly related to the book. There are also additional sites and several books that are about sports and athletes.

Websites

CBS Sports Line

http://cbs.sportsline.com

Contains daily information on a variety of sports, plus many sports-related links.

ESPN SportsZone

http://espn.sportszone.com

Home page of the sports television network with sports updates, scores, and news.

Information Please Sports Almanac

http://www.infoplease.com/sports.html

An almanac on a variety of sports with information that can be used in a variety of settings.

Jerry Spinelli Biography

http://www.carr.lib.md.us/authco/spinelli-j.htm

Author information with a list of other books by Jerry Spinelli and an audio message from the author.

Maniac Magee

http://lupus.northern.edu:90/hastingw/spinelli.html

This *Maniac Magee* web page features a look at some of the themes presented in the book. Information is provided on how to use and extend the themes in a classroom situation.

Maniac Magee

http://library.thinkquest.org/J001776/magee.html

From this site, students can take a quiz pertaining to the book *Maniac Magee*.

Maniac Magee by Jerry Spinelli

http://www.carr.lib.md.us/authco/spi-man.htm

Short introduction to *Maniac Magee* with a link to longer author information.

Maniac Magee by Jerry Spinelli

http://www.carolhurst.com/titles/maniacmagee.html

Educational activities centered around *Maniac Magee*. Includes a review of the book, cast of characters, activities, and list of related books.

National Baseball Hall of Fame

http://www.baseballhalloffame.org

Home page of the National Baseball Hall of Fame in Cooperstown, New York.

Sport! Science @ The Exploratorium

http://www.exploratorium.edu/sports/index.html

Sports and science in one nice package. Includes lots of fun and educational activities.

Sports Illustrated for Kids

http://www.sikids.com

Sports page designed just for kids with sporting information, news, and fun.

Books

Bowman-Kruhm, Mary. ***A Day in the Life of a Coach.*** Rosen, 1996. Part of The Kids' Career Library series, this volume presents shows children the challenges and rewards of coaching.

Gunderman, Meghann. ***I'm a Kid ...Run With Me! A Runner's Log & Diary for Young People.*** Sports Media Challenge, 1995. Written by a child as a training guide for children who like to run. The author was the 1993 North Carolina Schoolgirl Athlete of the Year.

Krull, Kathleen. ***Lives of the Athletes: Thrills, Spills (& What the Neighbors Thought).*** Harcourt Brace, 1997. Biographies of athletes written for children in grades 3–6.

Pare, Michael A. ***Sports Stars II, 2nd Ed.*** Gale, 1996. Biographical and informational accounts of a variety of athletes.

Scholastic Encyclopedia of Sports in America. Scholastic, 1997. American sports for kids in a very accessible encyclopedia format.

Track & Field. Chelsea House, 1998. An overview of track and field for children. Intended for grades 3 and up.

LQ12

Missing May
By Cynthia Rylant
Atheneum, 1991 • Newbery Medal, 1993

Introduction

Summer has lived with her Aunt May and Uncle Ob since she was six years old. Now, Aunt May has died, and Summer, Uncle Ob and Summer's friend Cletus begin a strange trip to search of May's spirit.

Assignment

Missing May is a story of generations, communication, and love. Relating to our elders is sometimes a difficult task. With understanding and a little help, we can learn from our elders, gain information about the past, and have fun.

Internet Resources

Intergenerational programming is a good way to bring children and their elders together. The Internet has many resources that explain intergenerational programs and provide information on the types of programs that have been done in the U.S. Use the following Internet resources for information and programming ideas.

Connecting the Generations: Linking Young & Old

   http://www.gu.org/proglinky&o.htm *Activities 1 & 2*

Intergenerational Programs

   http://www.sdcs.k12.ca.us/partners/Intergenerational_Program.htm *Activity 3*

Developing an Intergenerational Program

   http://www.cyfc.umn.edu/Parenting/Familylife/intergenerational.html *Activities 4 & 5*

Activities

1. What is an intergenerational program?

2. What are three things that intergenerational programming does for its participants?

3. What are four ways intergenerational programs bring old and young people together?

4. What are the basic features of successful intergenerational programming?

5. What four objectives should be considered in designing an intergenerational program?

Additional Activity

As part of your learning, design an intergenerational program. Your participants will be a senior citizen who is volunteering her time at the local public library, and a fourth grade child who is visiting the library for an afterschool program. The program you design will meet once a week for one month. It is your task to design the program, activities which will take place during each meeting, and learning goals to be achieved. Don't forget such details as time of day the program will take place, location, and resources. Present your findings to the class. For additional information on intergenerational programming, look in the "Educator Notes" section of this LearningQuest.

Conclusion

Intergenerational programs are a good way to bring youth and their elders together with a common goal. Not only can it be an educational experience, but the participants can have fun and form lasting friendships. Perhaps one day you will become involved in an intergenerational program or help develop such a program for children you know.

Educator Notes

Additional information about intergenerational programs can be found on the listed websites or in the resource books.

Websites

Author: Cynthia Rylant
http://strobe.lights.com/novel/generated/author/155.html
Short biographical sketch. Information on this site is similar to that on the previous site.

Cynthia Rylant
http://www.tetranet.net/users/stolbert/research/rylant.html
Very useful annotated bibliography and pathfinder. Contains good information for an author study.

Cynthia Rylant
http://falcon.jmu.edu/~ramseyil/rylant.htm
Biographical information on Cynthia Rylant. Good for classroom or library.

Developing an Interngenerational Program
http://www.cyfc.umn.edu/Parenting/Familylife/intergenerational.html
Offers intergenerational programming between college students and their elders. Contains useful background information.

Generations Together

http://www.pitt.edu/~gti

An Intergenerational Studies Program at the University of Pittsburgh.

Intergenerational Education Program

http://www.cde.ca.gov/cyfsbranch/lsp/intrfact.htm

Fact sheet on an existing intergenerational program. Includes description, overview, and purpose.

Intergenerational Programming

http://ohioline.osu.edu/ss-fact/0142.html

This article provides information on intergenerational programming and offers suggestions that could be used in a classroom situation.

Missing May

http://www.bdd.com

Use author search to find a synopsis of *Missing May.* Provides good background information on this book.

Roots & Wings Excursions

http://www.roots-wings.com/text/lifeskillscenter/index.htm

Family travel page which develops travel adventures for all generations. Any family combinations are encouraged.

Books

Bavasch, E. Barrie. ***Seminole Children & Elders Talk Together.*** Rosen Publishing Group, 1997. Part of the Library of Intergenerational Learning series.

Kavasch, E. Barrie. ***Seminole Children & Elders Talk Together.*** Rosen Publishing Group, 1997. A book in which Seminole elders share their lives.

Maricondi, Amy. ***Intergenerational Sharing & Caring: Developing & Maintaining an Adopt-a-Grandparent Program in Your Community.*** American Literary Press, 1995. Practical advice for those working on an intergenerational program in which children and elders form an ongoing relationship.

Newman, Sally. ***Intergenerational Programs: Past, Present & Future.*** Hemisphere Publishing, 1997. Intergenerational relations between various groups. Contains research-based applications, but some of the materials can be adapted for use with children.

Roehlkepartain, Lolene L. ***Creating Intergenerational Community: 75 Ideas for Building Relationships Between Youth & Adults.*** Search Institute, 1996. Practical guide for program development.

Island of the Blue Dolphins

By Scott O'Dell

Houghton Mifflin, 1960 • Newbery Medal, 1961

Introduction

Twelve-year-old Karana dives from a ship into the sea and swims back to the Island of the Blue Dolphins in search of her brother. As she waits for the ship to return, years pass. She spends her time gathering food, building shelter, and living her life on the island.

Assignment

As you read *Island of the Blue Dolphins*, think about the sea mammals for which the island is named. Dolphins are interesting and entertaining creatures. During this assignment, you will discover facts and information about dolphins.

Internet Resources

Bottlenose Dolphin: Physical Characteristics

> http://www.seaworld.org/infobooks/Bottlenose/phychardol.html *Activities 1 & 2*

Bottlenose Dolphins: Adaptions for an Aquatic Environment

> http://www.seaworld.org/infobooks/Bottlenose/adapaqdol.html *Activities 3 & 4*

Some Dolphin Basics

> http://ourworld.compuserve.com/homepages/jaap/dolphfaq.htm *Activities 5 & 6*

Activities

1. What is the average length and weight of bottlenose dolphins found off Florida?

2. What are a dolphin's forelimbs called? What is the main use of this forelimb?

3. What is the average depth a bottlenose dolphin will dive? What is the deepest trained dive for a bottlenose dolphin?

4. How does a dolphin breathe?
5. Where is the dorsal fin located?
6. What are the other two types of fins, and their purpose?

Additional Activity

As part of your learning, draw a dolphin and label the following body parts:

eye, blowhole, pectoral flipper, tail fluke, dorsal fin

Use the information you've found in the Internet Resources and those listed in Educator Notes to prepare a report on dolphins. Present your findings to your class. Interesting items you may wish to include in the report are feeding habits, size, coloration, swimming, or behavior.

Conclusion

Often we see dolphins who have been trained to entertain an audience. Dolphins are trainable and a lot of research has been conducted into the lives of these marine mammals. During this lesson, you've been exposed to some of the information which is known about dolphins. Perhaps you will have the opportunity to find additional information and facts about these mammals.

Educator notes

Additional Internet Resources and literature are listed below. Both types of resources contain valuable and useful information about dolphins which can be adapted to classroom use. In addition, Internet sites devoted to Scott O'Dell and cyberguides for *Island of the Blue Dolphins* are included in the list.

Websites

Blue Dolphin Bookscape

http://www.ctnba.org/ctn/k8/island.html

A "bookscape" for *Island of the Blue Dolphins.* (A bookscape is similar to a LearningQuest.)

Bottlenose Dolphins: Communication and Echolocation

http://www.seaworld.org/infobooks/Bottlenose/echodol.html

Provides information on communication and echolocation. This website is created by Sea World.

Dolphins

http://www.ncsa.uiuc.edu/edu/Affiliates/Elgin/GRANT/dolphpg.htm

Provides links for information on dolphins, including a dolphin art gallery, dolphin homepages, and other dolphin links.

Dolphins Plus Online!

http://www.pennekamp.com/dolphins-plus

Home page of a marine mammal research and educational center in Key Largo, Florida.

Island of the Blue Dolphins
http://www.ncsa.uiuc.edu/edu/Affiliates/Elgin/GRANT/pract.htm
Useful links for dolphins, the Aleut Indians, sea otters, Scott O'Dell, and book reviews.

Island of the Blue Dolphins
http://www.connectingstudents.com/literacy/dolphin.htm
This web page is designed for use by educators who wish to enhance the reading of *Island of the Blue Dolphins*. A list of lessons plans and resources for the book is provided, with many useful classroom activities.

Latin Lingo
http://www.seaworld.org/infobooks/Bottlenose/48activitydol.html
Offers a classroom activity featuring dolphins. Designed for students in grades 4–8.

Scott O'Dell
http://www.widomaker.com/~ganderson/scott.htm
Information on the Scott O'Dell Historical Fiction Award. Winners of the award are books which have been published in English by a U.S. publisher and set in North, South, or Central America.

Teachers@Random—The Novels of Scott O'Dell
http://www.randomhouse.com/teachers/guides/noso.html
Includes teaching ideas, reviews, author, and book information.

Teachers@Random—Scott O'Dell
http://www.randomhouse.com/teachers/authors/odel.html
Includes author information. Good for students who wish additional information on this popular author.

USM de Grummond Collection—Scott O'Dell Papers
http://www.lib.usm.edu/~degrum/findaids/odell.htm
Offers background on the Scott O'Dell Papers located in the de Grummond Collection at the University of Southern Mississippi.

Books

Bernard, Stephan. ***Interactive Dolphins.*** Scholastic, 1997. A fun look at dolphins with good information for use in educational settings.

Corrigan, Patricia. ***Dolphins for Kids.*** NorthWord, 1995. Part of the Wildlife for Kids series.

Pringle, Laurence. ***Dolphin Man: Exploring the World of Dolphins.*** Atheneum, 1995. Photography and factual insight into the world of dolphins. Photos done by the Dolphin Biology Research Institute.

Sanchez, Isidro. ***Dolphins: Animals With Sonar.*** Gareth Stevens, 1996. Highlights the sonar device used by dolphins. Designed for grades 3 and up.

Twinn, Michael. ***Great Dolphin.*** Child's Play, 1997. Informative book on dolphins for juveniles.

Dear Mr. Henshaw

By Beverly Cleary

Morrow, 1983 • Newbery Medal, 1984

Introduction

Leigh is a boy who writes stories, has a pen pal, and is interested in a lot of ideas. Leigh is also a boy who misses his father, who is on the road in his truck for long periods of time. Leigh's thoughts and feelings are expressed in the letters he writes to Mr. Henshaw, who is the author of Leigh's favorite book.

Assignment

In this unit, you will discover some information about letter writing, be exposed to the correct techniques for writing a formal letter, and read what others think of letter writing.

Internet Resources

After reading *Dear Mr. Henshaw*, use the Internet resources listed below to answer questions about letter writing. Think about the letters that Leigh wrote to Mr. Henshaw, and imagine what it would be like to have a pen pal who was a famous author.

Letter Writing

> http://education.umn.edu/SPS/career/ltrwrite.html *Activity 1*

An Extremely Abbreviated History of Letter-Writing

> http://www.beloit.edu/~amerdem/students/morrow2.html *Activities 2 & 3*

Eight or Nine Wise Words About Letter Writing: How to Begin a Letter

> http://www.hoboes.com/html/FireBlade/Carroll/Words/Letters2.html *Activity 4*

Eight or Nine Wise Words About Letter Writing: How to End a Letter

> http://www.hoboes.com/html/FireBlade/Carroll/Words/Letters4.html *Activity 5*

Kids.Com Keypal

http://www.kidscom.com/cgi-bin/keypal/keypal_search.pl *Activity 6*

Activities

1. What are two commandments for writing formal letters to make them readable?

2. How did the Sumerians communicate in 3500 BC?

3. What caused an increase in letter-writing?

4. When responding to a letter that has been written to you, what is a good way to begin that letter?

5. List four ways to end a letter.

6. Provide four rules of netiquette for use when writing letters or corresponding via e-mail.

Additional Activity

Keypals allow children and adults to correspond with others via the Internet. There are numerous ways to find a keypal, including the Internet addresses listed below. With the supervision of your teacher, choose one of the Internet addresses and begin a keypal experience. After you have corresponded with someone for at least two weeks, provide a report for your class. Present the class with an update of your activities after two months of correspondence. Have your "letters" changed? In what way have they changed? What have you learned from this experience?

Key Pals Global Connections

http://www.learningspace.org/ric/gprojects/ricglobal.html

eMail Classroom Exchange

http://www.epals.com

Intercultural E-Mail Classroom Connections

http://www.iecc.org

Conclusion

Letter writing has long been a vital aspect of communication. With the invention of the typewriter, computers, and the World Wide Web, letter writing has changed, but it's still very important. Sometimes penpals will continue to exchange letters for numerous years. Hopefully you will achieve the same type of friendship via your keypal exchange.

Educator Notes

The following is a list of Internet sites and books which provide additional information on letter writing. There are many keypal sites available which can be accessed for classroom use. Using the search term "keypal" will provide numerous Internet sites.

Websites

Beverly Cleary

http://www.davison.k12.mi.us/dms/projects/women/acleary.htm

Includes biographical information, awards, trivia, and a bibliography for this famous, much-read author.

Beverly Cleary

http://www.edupaperback.org/authorbios/Cleary_Beverly.html

Offers a brief biography of Beverly Cleary as presented by The Educational Paperback Association.

The Beverly Cleary Home Page

http://www.d.umn.edu/~yyang2/beverly_cleary.html

This is an extensive and fun site for Beverly Cleary fans.

Beverly Cleary Teacher Resource Center

http://falcon.jmu.edu/~ramseyil/cleary.htm

Includes author information, additional links for lesson plans, and a list of sites on Beverly Clearly.

ELA Elementary Level: Letter Writing

http://www.sasked.gov.sk.ca/docs/ela/ela_lett.html

Includes the purpose and procedures for letter writing. Suited for use with young children.

Effective Letter Writing

http://www.greencis.net/~shart/letter.html

Encourages letter writing to gain genealogical facts and stories and includes letter writing techniques for discovering family information.

Eight or Nine Wise Words About Letter Writing: How to Go On with a Letter

http://www.hoboes.com/html/FireBlade/Carroll/Words/Letters3.html

Offers information for writing the body of a letter, including tips, hints, and letter-writing rules.

How to Write a Letter to the Editor

http://thearc.org/ga/letr2ed.html

Provides tips on effective letters to a newspaper editor. The information provided can be used in any size newspaper, and offers suggestions for making your opinions printable.

How to Write a Letter to Your Legislator

http://www.faribault.k12.mn.us/admin/How%20to%20write.htm

Offers advice on writing to a legislator, as suggested in part by the American Library Association.

Letter-Writing—A Dying Art?

http://www.beloit.edu/~amerdem/students/morrow1.html

Background information and importance of letter writing. Includes a link to the history of letter writing.

Meet Beverly Cleary

http://teacher.scholastic.com/authorsandbooks/authors/cleary/bio.htm

Provides biographical information, links to books by Beverly Cleary, and classroom activities.

Newspapers in the Classroom: Grade 5, Letters to the Editor

http://cam.scdsb.on.ca/letters5.htm

Provides a lesson plan for writing letters to a newspaper editor with activities, summary, and evaluation questions.

A Pen Pal Experience

http://www.challenge.state.la.us/k12act/data/penpal-exp.html

Offers a language arts lesson plan for a pen pal unit. Target grade level: 4.

SCORE: Teacher Guide: Dear Mr. Henshaw

http://www.sdcoe.k12.ca.us/score/dear/deartg.html

This page is an educational supplement for *Dear Mr. Henshaw*, including information found via the Internet.

Books

Cobb, Nancy. ***Letter Writer Book & Stationary Set.*** Reader's Digest Young Families, 1994. Letter writing for children, including composition exercises.

Goodman, Ruth F. ***Pen Pals: What It Means to Be Jewish in Israel & America.*** Fithian Press, 1996. Fictional account of pen pals across the miles.

James, Elizabeth. ***Sincerely Yours: How to Write Great Letters.*** Houghton Mifflin, 1993. Effective tools for use when writing letters. Composition and letter writing for children in grades 4–8.

Kroeker, Suze M. ***Power Penning: A Student's Guide to Letter Writing Success.*** Manchester House Publishing, 1996. Language and composition exercises for letter writing. Designed for use with older children, but some activities can be adapted for use with younger groups.

Willing, Kathlene. ***Partnerships for Classroom Learning: From Reading Buddies to Pen Pals to the Community & World Beyond.*** Heinemann, 1996. Activity ideas for the elementary classroom on using pen pals to foster understanding.

LQ15

M.C. Higgins, The Great

By Virginia Hamilton

Macmillan, 1974 • Newbery Medal, 1975

Introduction

Young M.C .Higgins does not understand his father's love for the family land. Although M.C. fears the slag heap which is threatening his home, with his mother's songs, father's devotion, and family love, M.C. learns the meaning of "home."

Assignment

M.C. Higgins, the Great is a story in which music plays an important role. M.C.'s mother has a voice of excellent quality, and M.C. believes she will make records one day in Nashville. Through the songs of M.C.'s mother, the reader and M.C. learn the meaning of "home." Through this unit, you will learn some songwriting tips, musical notes, and essential elements of music.

Internet Resources

Songwriting Article

http://www.suite101.com/articles/article.cfm/4071 *Activities 1 & 2*

Call/Response

http://hum.lss.wisc.edu/jazz/call.response.html *Activity 3*

Scale

http://www.hnh.com/NewDesign/fglossary.files/bglossary.files/Scale.htm *Activity 4*

Octave

http://www.hnh.com/NewDesign/fglossary.files/bglossary.files/Octave.htm *Activity 5*

Essential Elements of Music

http://www2.tltc.ttu.edu/Tanner/Presentations/begv/index.htm   *Activity 6*

Activities

1. What are two components used in building a song?

2. Use the link that is provided at the website, and list three ABCs of songwriting.

3. How is "Call and Response" music sung?

4. What is a Scale?

5. What is the definition of Octave?

6. What is the Tonal Ladder?

Additional Activity

There are many types of music, both vocal and instrumental. If you play an instrument, prepare a short song to present to your class. If you'd rather, sing a song or teach the class an action song using differing actions to represent the words of the song. To learn additional information about music, go to the following site and click on the links to listen to various notes.

The Basics of Reading Music

http://members.home.net/kmeixner/music/readingmusic.htm

Conclusion

Music is a way of communicating, telling stories, sharing thoughts, feelings, and ideas. You do not need to be a good singer or play a musical instrument to enjoy music. All that you really need is the time to listen and enjoy what you hear.

Educator Notes

There are numerous sites on the Internet for music educators. The following is a selected list. A short bibliography representative of music books for use with children is included.

Websites

Children's Music Web

http://www.childrensmusic.org

Provides numerous musical links, including educational links and sites for fun.

The History of the Trapp Family

http://www.trappfamily.com/history.html

Presents information about the musical family on which *The Sound of Music* is based.

Irene Jackson: Songwriting Tips

http://www.islandnet.com/~woloshen/tips.html

Provides tips and information for all who write (or want to write) songs.

K-12 Resources For Music Educators

http://www.isd77.k12.mn.us/resources/staffpages/shirk/k12.music.html

This page offers an extensive list of sites for music educators. Many of the links contain lesson plans, activities, or classroom ideas.

Lullabies and Other Songs for Children

http://www.kididdles.com

Provides words to children's songs with an alphabetical index, song of the week, and related links.

Viriginia Hamilton

http://falcon.jmu.edu/~ramseyil/hamilton.htm

Includes author information and bibliography. A good educational site.

Virginia Hamilton

http://www.virginiahamilton.com

This is the home page of Virginia Hamilton with information for all fans of Ms. Hamilton and her books.

WebChoir

http://brainop.media.mit.edu/online/net-music/WebMusic/choir.html

This interactive musical site allows the user to determine vocal range.

Books

Ardley, Neil. ***A Young Person's Guide to Music: A Listener's Guide.*** D K Publishing, 1995. Music analysis and appreciation for children. Good for use with students in grades 4–9.

Burton, Leon. ***Adventures in Music Listening: Level 1 Big Book.*** Warner, 1996. Music appreciation for children. Also includes information on music analysis.

Discovering Music. Voyetra Technologies, 1995. Musical history, analysis, appreciation, and criticism. Includes a CD-ROM.

Kaufman, Elizabeth. ***Bipquiz: Music.*** Sterling, 1997. Question and answer book of music for children. A fun book which can be used in a unit of study about music.

Wilson, Clive. ***The Kingfisher Young People's Book of Music.*** Larousse Kingfisher Chambers, 1996. Musical history and criticism. Children ages 9–13 should find useful information on a variety of music here.

LQ16

Walk Two Moons

By Sharon Creech

HarperCollins, 1994 • Newbery Medal, 1995

Introduction

Salamanca Tree Hiddle begins a cross-country trip with her grandparents to visit her mother in Idaho. Along the way, Sal entertains her grandparents with stories about her friend Phoebe, and in the process begins to learn about herself and her mother.

Assignment

As Sal and her grandparents travel, they visit many tourist attractions along the way. Their trip offers them the opportunity to spend time together and see many interesting sights. Taking a trip is an activity which is enjoyed by many. During this LearningQuest, you will have the opportunity to visit places in our country via the Internet, plan a trip, and learn about maps.

Internet Resources

After reading *Walk Two Moons,* think what it would be like to take a trip across the U.S. By visiting the following Internet resources and answering the assigned questions, you will become a participant in an exciting trip.

MapQuest! TripQuest

> http://www.mapquest.com *Activities 1 & 2*

National Park Foundation, Badlands National Park

> http://www.nationalparks.org/guide/parks/badlands-nat-1924.htm *Activity 3*

The Total Yellowstone Page

> http://www.yellowstone-natl-park.com/address.htm *Activity 4*

Fantastic Journeys: Old Faithful

> http://www.nationalgeographic.com/features/97/yellowstone/catch/index.html
> *Activities 5 & 6*

Activities

1. Click the link for "TripQuest." Follow the directions and type your home address as the starting point and 1600 Pennsylvania Avenue, Washington DC, as the destination. Using the City to City directions, how many miles will you travel were you to take this trip? How many states would you pass through on this trip?

2. Now, click the link for "Interactive Atlas." Type your home address, city, state, and zip code to make a map of your area. Is the map accurate? Is anything important missing? Could you use this map to provide directions to your home?

3. What are the driving directions to the Badlands National Park Ben Reifel Visitor Center?

4. What is the address of Yellowstone National Park? What is the email address for the park?

5. Approximately how often does Old Faithful erupt?

6. Is Old Faithful really "faithful?" Why or why not?

Additional Activity

Visiting different parts of our country can be a fun and educational experience. We form new impressions of people and places that we visit. What is a favorite area that you have visited? Using an Internet search engine, see if you can find information about the place you have visited. Prepare information for your class on the area you have chosen to research. Also include information from reference books in the library. You may wish to include a map to help your classmates visualize the area you have chosen.

Conclusion

Traveling is an exciting way to learn. In *Walk Two Moons,* Sal and her grandparents set out on a journey that teaches them about themselves and brings them closer as a family. A trip does not have to be a long drive across country to have merit. Sometimes the best journeys are the short car trips that are taken as a family.

Educator notes

The World Wide Web features many websites about national parks and traveling. The following is a brief list. Additional information can be found in the books at the end of the listing.

Websites

ALCS: About Sharon Creech

http://www.ala.org/alsc/creech.html

Provides biographical information about Sharon Creech. This site has good information for an author study.

ALCS: 1995 Newbery Medal Winner

http://www.ala.org/alsc/N1995.html

This page has official information about the 1995 Newbery Medal-winning and Honor books from the American Library Association.

Berit's Best Sites for Children: World Travel

http://db.cochran.com/li_showElems:theoPage:theo:4940:0.db

Provides many travel links chosen specifically for children. Excellent resource with good variety.

Creech Awarded for Kids' Book

http://wildcat.arizona.edu/papers/old-wildcats/spring95/February/February7,1995/09_2_m.html

This page is a newspaper article announcing Sharon Creech as winner of the Newbery Medal.

Fun and Games: How Far?

http://academic.brooklyn.cuny.edu/geology/leveson/core/linksa/scalequiz1a.html

A short quiz on distance is presented on this web page. Students will have the opportunity to extend learning on using maps by answering the questions posed.

National Park Information Center

http://www.americanparks.com/

This web page features a park locator, information on the National Park Service and a "National Park of the Month."

Rand McNally K12 Online

http://www.k12online.com/

A good site for educators who wish to incorporate travel and maps into the classroom curriculum. Featured are a teacher's corner, activities, and links for educators.

Rand McNally Explore America

http://www.randmcnally.com/rmc/explore/exploreMain.jsp?

This page offers travel news by U.S. regions. Includes special events, weather, travel guides, and travel tips.

Sharon Creech

http://www.harpercollins.com/authors/pages/creech_sharon.htm

This publisher page provides information on *Walk Two Moons*.

World Surfari

http://www.supersurf.com

Visit different countries, learning about the history, people, and society. A fun geographical site for kids.

Books

Bramwell, Martyn. **How Maps Are Made.** Lerner, 1997. Information on cartography, maps, and map drawing.

Julio, Susan. **Great Map Mysteries.** Scholastic, 1997. Mysteries of maps for use with children. This would be a good curriculum extender.

Kenda, Margaret and Phyllis S. Williams. **Geography Wizard for Kids.** Barron's Educational Series, 1997. Maps and fun for children. Intended for use with children ages 8–12.

Rand McNally Staff. **Are We There Yet? Backseat Books.** Rand McNally, 1996. Travel activities for children from this well-known map source.

The Reader's Digest Children's Atlas of the World. Reader's Digest Young Families, 1997. A world atlas for children. This would be a good title to use with a group.

Whitman, Sylvia. **Get Up & Go: The History of American Road Travel.** Lerner, 1996. A children's guide to the history of travel and transportation.

Wright, David and Jill Wright. **Facts on File Children's Atlas.** Facts on File, 1997. An atlas designed for children grades 4–9.

The Hero and the Crown

By Robin McKinley

Greenwillow, 1984 • Newbery Medal, 1985

Introduction

Aerin is a daughter of destiny. She is destined to become a heroine who will carry the power of the Blue Sword. Along the way, Aerin fights many personal and heroic battles. This story is one which will take readers into the world of knights, dragons, and magic.

Assignment

One of the most colorful and exciting stories in history is the tale of King Arthur and His Roundtable. The story of Arthur is considered by some to be a mixture of fact and fiction. In this LearningQuest, you will discover information about King Arthur, and life during this period in time.

Internet Resources

Camelot
> http://uidaho.edu/student_orgs/arthurian_legend/england/sites/camelot.htm
> *Activity 1*

Arthurian Origins
> http://uidaho.edu/student_orgs/arthurian_legend/origins/arthur.html   *Activity 2*

Arthurian Britain
> http://www.britannia.com/history/timearth.html   *Activity 3*

People of the Middle Ages
> http://www.byu.edu/ipt/projects/middleages/LifeTimes/People.html   *Activity 4*

Did You Know
> http://www.byu.edu/ipt/projects/middleages/LifeTimes/Tidbits.html   *Activity 5*

LearningQuest 17 : The Hero and the Crown

Flags/Banners

http://www.byu.edu/ipt/projects/middleages/LifeTimes/Banners.html *Activity 6*

Activities

1. What are two possible sites of Camelot?

2. What are two possible theories that explain the legend of Arthur?

3. When was Arthur supposedly born?

4. Who were the knights? At what age would a squire become a knight?

5. What was the invention which aided the knight on horseback? When did this invention arrive in India?

6. What are four types of flags used in the Middle Ages?

Additional Activity

Life during the time of Arthur was exciting, adventurous, and at times dangerous. As a creative writing project, recreate Arthur and place him in our times. What type of person would Arthur be? Who would be his knights? Describe Camelot and the activities of the Roundtable. You may wish to provide a floor plan of Arthur's castle and the materials used in battle. Share your project with your classmates.

Conclusion

The Middle Ages and the legends of Arthur have long held the interest of many people. As legends continue, they change, develop, and become more widespread. Do you think Arthur was an actual person? Why or why not? Is there someone you know that you think would be like Arthur? Who is that person, and why do they remind you of Arthur?

Educator Notes

The websites and books listed here have additional information on music, games, health, and daily life during the Middle Ages. There are also additional resources about King Arthur and and his Round Table knights.

Websites

Arthurian Legend

http://www.uidaho.edu/student_orgs/arthurian_legend/quests/monsters/adrgpg.html
Provides a section on King Arthur and dragons.

Arthurian Sites in England

http://www.uidaho.edu/student_orgs/arthurian_legend/england/sites/camelot.htm

This site shows Arthurian places in Scotland, Wales, and England.

Bards, Music, and Arthurian Legend

http://www.uidaho.edu/student_orgs/arthurian_legend/game/music/arthur.htm

Music in the time of King Arthur. The information at this site includes some early examples of Arthurian music in Great Britain and Celtic tunes in MIDI file format.

Hangman

http://www.uidaho.edu/student_orgs/arthurian_legend/game/music/Hangman.html

Play the Arthurian version of the well-known game "Hangman."

The Hero and the Crown

http://ofb.net/~damien/mckinley/HeroCrown/

This is a list of reviews and a discussion from when *The Hero and the Crown* was awarded the Newbery Medal.

Middle Ages Internet Links

http://www.byu.edu/ipt/projects/middleages/WEBSites.html

Offers links for art, King Arthur, culture, and literature. Many of these links will lead the student to additional Internet sites on Medieval Europe.

The Middle Ages

http://www.byu.edu/ipt/projects/middleages/Intro.html

Contains information and additional links to the Middle Ages and King Arthur. An extensive site which would work well for additional LearningQuest questions or activities.

The Middle Ages—Arts & Entertainment

http://www.learner.org/exhibits/middleages/artsentr.html

Listen to medieval music and contribute to a medieval story. Provides background music and songs.

The Middle Ages—Feudal Life

http://www.learner.org/exhibits/middleages/feudal.html

Provides an overview to life during the Middle Ages. Presented by the Annenberg/CPB Project Exhibits Collection.

The Middle Ages—Health: Medieval Medicine

http://www.learner.org/exhibits/middleages/healtact2.html

You decide the treatment for a variety of medieval ailments. Contains a link for additional information on symptoms and healing methods.

The Middle Ages—Related Resources

http://www.learner.org/exhibits/middleages/related.html

Provides numerous links for the Middle Ages, including a dictionary of feudal terms, medieval Europe, and related literature.

Official Robin McKinley Home Page

http://ofb.net/~damien/mckinley

Biographical information, readers' survey section, and information about Robin McKinley's books.

The Quest

http://www.uidaho.edu/student_orgs/arthurian_legend/welcome.html

This extensive site of Arthurian information, includes origins of Arthurian legends, fun and games, Camelot, knights, and Arthurian art.

Robin McKinley

http://www.robinmckinley.com/

This page provides good biographical information about Robin McKinley. Includes a list of reference books with further information on Ms. McKinley and her books.

Books

Dixon-Kennedy, Mike. ***Heroes of the Round Table.*** Blandford, 1997. Legends and history of Arthurian times with a bibliography of additional resources.

McCaughrean, Geraldine. ***King Arthur and the Round Table.*** Macdonald Young, 1996. The story of King Arthur, presented for children. A good source.

Morpurgo, Michael. ***Arthur, High King of Britain.*** Mammoth, 1997. A retelling of nine familiar tales about Arthur and his knights.

Steeden, Caroline. ***The First book of King Arthur.*** Parragon, 1997. Includes information about Arthur, knights and knighthood, and Arthur's sword, Excalibur.

Talbott, Hudson. ***King Arthur and the Round Table.*** Morrow Junior Books, 1995. Retelling of the story of how Arthur becomes King, and the beginnings of the Knights of the Round Table.

Williams, Marcia. ***King Arthur and the Knights of the Round Table.*** Candlewick Press, 1997. Based on Sir Thomas Malory's *Le Morte d'Arthur.* Presents legends, folklore, and Arthurian stories.

Yolen, Jane ***Merlin and the Dragons.*** Cobblehill, 1997. A story of Arthur and Merlin, done in braille. Braille and print pages appear alternately.

The Door in the Wall
By Marguertie de Angeli
Doubleday, 1949 • Newbery Medal, 1950

Introduction

Robin is the son of a nobleman, and his future has been decided for him because of the circumstances of his birth. Robin must become a knight, but due to unforeseen events, Robin's life is changed forever.

Assignment

The Door in the Wall is a story of people and places. A castle was an important place during the time period of this story. The castle was more than a place of residence. Often, entire communities were dependent upon the castle and those who lived within its walls. During this LearningQuest, you will discover information about castles and their functions.

Internet Resources

What is a Castle?

> http://www.castlewales.com/cast_def.html *Activities 1 & 2*

Ian's Land of Castles

> http://www.personal.psu.edu/faculty/n/x/nxd10/castles.htm *Activities 3, 4 & 5*

Castles on the Web Glossary

> http://fox.nstn.ca/~tmonk/castle/glossary.html *Activity 6*

Activities

1. According to the *Oxford English Dictionary*, what is the definition of a castle? From what languages is the word "castle" derived?

2. What are three functions of a castle?

3. Why were castles made?

4. What were early castles called?

5. How was a castle under siege protected?

6. Define the following terms:

arcade

arch

bailey

bastion

drawbridge

fresco

gable

gallery

keep

lancet

moat

postern gate

Additional Activity

Design your own castle. Be sure to include living areas, work space, and other necessary rooms or areas of the castle. You may wish to think about the number of people who will be living in the castle and how to provide for their food, clothing, and living needs. Draw a floor plan of your castle, labeling each room. You can design your castle using poster board and markers, or create a three-dimensional castle. Share your castle with your class.

Conclusion

Castles represent an interesting time in the history of our world. Often castles are related to kings and queens, but castles were also places of work, government, and learning. Each is different, as are the stories which are told about them. Through this LearningQuest, you have been exposed to the history of castles and the terminology associated with them. There are a lot of sites devoted to castles, kings, queens, and knights. In addition, numerous books on the subject have been published. To further your knowledge, try some of the resources listed in the Educator Notes of this LearningQuest.

Educator Notes

Further the learning of your students by using the Internet sites and books listed below. The list is a small representation of the information which is available about castles and related subjects.

Websites

Castles

http://csis.pace.edu/grendel/projs3h/castles.htm
Presents good information and a link to a medieval castle.

Castles of Europe
http://www.heartofeurope.com/castles.html
Information on castles in England, Scotland, Wales, France, Belgium, and the Netherlands.

The Castles of Wales
http://www.castlewales.com/home.html
Offers exploration of medieval castles in Wales, including specific castle maps and information.

Castle on the Web
http://fox.nstn.ca/~tmonk/castle/main.html
Includes castle tours, collections, castles for kids, and a castle quest game.

Castles on the Web
http://www.castlesontheweb.com/search/Castle_Tours/
This page features neat photos of castles and cathedrals in Europe.

Journey Through the Middle Ages with James the Jingling Jester
http://tqjunior.thinkquest.org/4051/titlepg.htm
Designed by 4th grade students, this site is packed with information and fun. An excellent resource.

Life in a Medieval Castle
http://www.castlewales.com/life.html
Provides information on different living areas of a castle, including the hall, kitchen, and domestic buildings.

Teachers@Random—The Door in the Wall
http://www.randomhouse.com/teachers/authors/door.html
This page is a teacher's guide for *The Door in the Wall*. Includes teaching ideas, classroom activities, and thematic connections.

Teachers@Random—Marguerite de Angeli
http://www.randomhouse.com/teachers/authors/dean.html
Provides author information and a link to further information about *The Door in the Wall*.

Wales, Land of Castles
http://www.data-wales.co.uk/castles1.htm
Offers information on some of the many castles in Wales. Also includes information on Wales, and the Cadw, which is charged with the preservation and promotion of castles in Wales.

Books

Day, Malcolm. ***The World of Castles & Forts.*** Peter Bedrick Books, 1996. Castles, forts, and the world surrounding the two subjects.

Nardo, Don. ***The Medieval Castle.*** Lucent Books, 1997. Middle Ages and castles.

Pipe, Jim. *Medieval **Castle.*** Millbrook Press, 1996. Presents typical activities in a castle for children in grades 4–6.

Wilkinson, Philip. ***Castles.*** D K, 1997. Book on the medieval time period and castles.

World Book Editors. ***Age of Knights & Castles.*** World Book, 1996. Information on castles, knights, and knighthood.

LQ19

The Midwife's Apprentice

By Karen Cushman

Clarion, 1995 • Newbery Medal, 1996

Introduction

Brat is a homeless girl with little reason to be hopeful about the future. With determination and a little luck, she becomes a midwife's apprentice and a person with a real name.

Assignment

Brat is given her name by the midwife because she does not have a true name. Our names are unique, because they identify us, provide us a history, and sometimes lend a clue to our lives. Through the use of the Internet, you will discover much about the meanings of names, the history of how some names are chosen, and have fun along the way.

Internet Resources

History of Names

    http://www.greencis.net/~shart/names.html *Activities 1 & 2*

Baby Naming

    http://babycenter.com/refcap/1505.html *Activity 3*

Popular Baby Names

    http://www.babycenter.com/babyname/popnames.html *Activities 4 & 5*

Baby Name Finder

    http://www.parentsoup.com/babynames/lookup *Activity 6*

Activities

1. What are the four main ways that family surnames are adopted? Explain each way.

2. When did parents first begin to give children a first and middle name?

3. What are four factors which some parents consider in choosing a name for their baby?

4. What was the most popular boy's name in 2001? What was the most popular girl's name?

5. What were the same names in 1930? Compare the two years.

6. Enter your name into the spaces provided. What is the origin of your first name? Middle? Last?

Additional Activity

Names are fun because they identify you and are unique. Interview your classmates and ask them the following questions about their names:

1. What is your full name?

2. Is there anyone in your family who has the same or similar name as you?

3. Do you have a nickname? If so, does your nickname relate to your real name? In what way?

4. If you could change your name, what would you like it to be? Why?

5. Do you know the meaning of your last name? If so, what does it mean? If you do not know the meaning of your last name, make up a meaning and explain your choice.

For the second part of the Additional Activity section, interview your parents using the same questions. Compare the two groups. Are there any similarities or differences? Why do you think your classmates provided the answers they did? Your parents? Share your findings with the class.

Conclusion

Our names are one of our identifying features. There are many types of names: family, historical, inventive, or poetic. No matter what your name, it is your name and can be used to identify you, give you character, and be a source of pride.

Educator notes

The Internet features numerous baby naming sites. Many of these provide information on the history of names or their popularity. Many books have been published on the topic as well. The following list can be used to develop additional learning situations for classroom use.

Websites

ALSC: 1996 Newbery Medal Winner

http://www.ala.org/alsc/N1996.html

This is the 1996 Newbery Medal and Honor Book site, sponsored by the American Library Association.

About Karen Cushman

http://www.ala.org/alsc/cushman.html

Offers bibliographic and literary information about the author of *The Midwife's Apprentice.*

About the Author

http://www.eduplace.com/rdg/author/cushman/aboutauthor.html

Includes biography, author links, 1996 Newbery Award acceptance speech, and an article by Cushman's husband.

Author Spotlight

http://www.eduplace.com/rdg/author/index.html

This site includes Karen Cushman information, including book summaries, articles, an author biography, and classroom activities.

Baby Name Finder

http://www.parentsoup.com/babynames/finder

Includes name origins and popular and unusual names. Users can also create the "perfect" name at this site.

Baby Names!

http://babynames.com

There are over 4,500 names in this particular Internet database. Also includes a list of popular names.

BabyZone: Baby Names!

http://www.babyzone.com/babynames/babynames.asp

Includes a name survey, name analyzer, definitions, and more.

Cushman

http://www.scils.rutgers.edu/special/kay/cushman5.html

This Karen Cushman site was written by an 8th grade student.

Cushman Page

http://www.scils.rutgers.edu/special/kay/cushman.html

Learn about Karen Cushman. This website is maintained by Kay E. Vandergrift at Rutgers.

In the Classroom

http://www.eduplace.com/rdg/author/cushman/classroom.html

Offers activities, literary elements, and cross-curricular connections, based on *The Midwife's Apprentice.*

Interview with Karen Cushman

http://www.eduplace.com/rdg/author/cushman/question.html

An interview with Karen Cushman using questions developed by readers of her books.

Midwife's Apprentice

http://www.soemadison.wisc.edu/ccbc/midwife.htm

This site contains reader feedback about the novel that originated from a discussion site.

The Midwife's Apprentice by Karen Cushman

http://www.carolhurst.com/titles/midwifesapprentice.html

This is a book review of *The Midwife's Apprentice*. The site is part of the Carol Hurst Web page, which presents a variety of educational activities.

Name Files

http://www.census.gov/genealogy/names

Provides information on most popular first and last names from the 1990 U.S. Census.

Names

http://babynames.com/namenu.htm

Input a name and receive the meaning of that name. A fun activity for kids and adults alike.

Newbery Medal Acceptance

http://www.eduplace.com/rdg/author/cushman/newbery.html

This page presents the 1996 Newbery Medal Acceptance Speech by Karen Cushman.

Popular Baby Names

http://www.independenthealth.com/

Provides a list of popular boy's and girl's names.

A Short Treatise on Anglo-Norman Personal Names

http://www.byu.edu/ipt/projects/middleages/LifeTimes/Names.html

Offers the historical aspect of names, with a list of names from medieval England and Germany.

TeacherView: The Midwife's Apprentice

http://www.eduplace.com/tview/tviews/m/midwifesapprentice.html

Teacher reactions and activities, including discussion and higher-level reasoning activities.

Books

Conings, Clayne. **Miracle of Names.** Sunstar Publishing, 1996. Descriptive analysis of given names. For use with older readers, but contains useful information.

Dunkling, Leslie. **The Guinness Book of Names,** **7th Ed.** Facts on File, 1995. Name information in dictionary/encyclopedic format.

Hook, J. N. **All These Wonderful Names: A Potpourri of People, Places & Things.** John Wiley & Sons, 1991. Names and places in history and present time.

Peterson, Sarah M. *The Book of Names: Over 1000 Biblical, Historical & Popular Names.* Tyndale House, 1997. A dictionary and reference guide of names.

Shanson, T. L. *International Guide to Names & Forms of Address.* Trans-Atlantic Publications, 1997. Provides information on names from other cultures.

Ingraham, Holly. *People's Names: A Cross-Cultural Reference Guide to the Proper Use of Over 40,000 Personal & Familial Names in Over 100 Cultures.* McFarland, 1997. Extensive book of first and last names from a variety of countries and cultures.

Muschell, David. *What In the Word? Origins of Words Dealing with People & Places.* McGuinn & McGuire Publishing, 1996. Geographical and personal names. Provides useful information on the origins of personal names.

Room, Adrian. *Cassell Dictionary of First Names.* Cassell Academic, 1997. Provides information on personal names. This volume will aid in research and discovery.

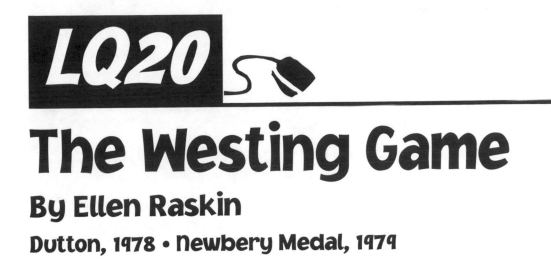

The Westing Game

By Ellen Raskin

Dutton, 1978 • Newbery Medal, 1979

Introduction

Sixteen heirs who all live in the same apartment building are provided the clues to solve the mystery of Sam Westing's death. Who really killed Sam Westing? And why?

Assignment

Solving a mystery is a lot like playing a game. You are provided clues or rules, and in order to win the game, you must follow the rules. In this LearningQuest, you will learn the history of some games, learn rules for others, and perhaps have some fun playing games on the World Wide Web.

Internet Resources

Playsite—Chess History
> http://www.playsite.com/t/games/board/chess/history.html *Activities 1 & 2*

Playsite—Chess Rules
> http://www.playsite.com/t/games/board/chess/rules.html *Activity 3*

Funbrain.com Fun Match Memory Game
> http://www.funbrain.com/match/index.html *Activity 4*

Funbrain: Educational Kids Games
> http://www.funbrain.com *Activity 5*

Puzzlemaker—Word Search
> http://puzzlemaker.school.discovery.com/WordSearchSetupForm.html *Activity 6*

Activities

1. What was the original name for chess?

2. When did the game evolve into its present-day form and rules?

3. How many people can play a chess game? How many playing pieces does each person have? What are those pieces?

4. Pick a symbol and difficulty level and play the memory game as directed. How successful were you? Did you enjoy this game? Why or why not?

5. Choose one of the games on this site. Play that game and compare your luck with a classmate who played the same game. How well did you do?

6. Generate a word search puzzle and complete the puzzle. Did you find all the words? In what format were some of the words presented in the puzzle? Backward? Sideways? Bottom to top? Other?

Additional Activity

All children and a lot of adults play games. Not only do we play games for fun, we can learn from games. Games teach us memory skills, cooperation with teammates, and give us the opportunity to develop new skills. Take a poll of your classmates and find what the most popular game is in your class. It can be an outdoor game or board game or card game. Rank the results in 1–5 order, with 5 being the most popular.

Conclusion

As you grow, you will play many different games. Some will be played outside, others with friends. Remember that each game has a history, rules, goals, and will teach you different skills. You can learn cooperation, athletic skill, sharpen your memory skills, and have fun, all while playing games.

Educator Notes

Games are an important part of learning. Often games can be used or adapted for the classroom curriculum. The following sites on the World Wide Web and books are useful resources for the classroom teacher, librarian, or parent.

Websites

Cyber Jacques' Cyber Seas Treasure Hunt

http://www.cyberjacques.com

Many online games for the entire family, including Fish, Tangram Puzzles, Connect the Dots, Hang Man, and Simon Says.

Four Square

http://www.corpcomm.net/~gnieboer/foursquare.htm

Rules for a game played in many schoolyards, which uses a kickball and grid painted on the ground.

Hide and Seek

http://www.corpcomm.net/~gnieboer/Hide_and_seek.htm

Rules for the classic game of childhood. Also includes a variation called Jail Break.

Memory Fish

http://www.thepuzzlefactory.com/memory/memfish.cfm

A fun game for kids to play on the Internet. This game requires Macromedia Shockwave plug-in installed on the computer.

Mother May I

http://www.corpcomm.net/~gnieboer/mother_may_i.html

Includes the rules and a variation for this childhood game.

Online Games, Puzzles, and Activities

http://smplanet.com/kids/games.html

Numerous links to Internet game sites. A good site with fun for all ages.

Puzzles and Games

http://www.kidinfo.com/Student_Leisure/Puzzles_and_Games.html

Puzzles and games on the Internet, including card games, board games, and word games.

Books

Warner, Penny. ***Games People Play: The Biggest & Best Book of Party Games & Activities.*** Simon & Schuster, 1998. A book of games, many of which are childhood favorites.

Drake, Jane. ***Kids Summer Games Book.*** General Distribution Services, 1998. Games for the hot days of summer or cold days of winter.

Middleton, Thomas H. ***Crostics: 50 Original Puzzles.*** Simon & Schuster, 1997. Crossword puzzles and games. Crossword puzzles are a great learning tool, which can work well in the classroom.

Cole, Joanna. ***The Any Day Book.*** William Morrow, 1997. Creative activities and seatwork that feature games. This book has a good variety of fun, educational activities.

Fleisher, Paul. ***Brain Food: Games That Make Kids Think.*** Zephyr Press, 1997. Perfect thinking recipe for school, library, or home.

McClaine, L. S. ***Games for Learning: A Curriculum Supplement for Homeschoolers.*** Nutmeg Publications, 1997. Games for homeschoolers. Can be adapted for use in any educational setting.

The Book of Classic Board Games. Klutz Press, 1996. The games we all love.

Out of the Dust

By Karen Hesse

Scholastic, 1997 • Newbery Medal, 1998

Introduction

Through the use of free verse poetry, fourteen-year-old Billie Joe tells the story of her life during the Great Depression. Her mother has died in an accident, which has also left Billie Joe unable to play the piano due to burns on her hands. Her resolve to move beyond tragedy, during a tragic time in our nation's history, brings Billie Joe out of the dust.

Assignment

The Great Depression was a time of emotional and financial turmoil in the United States. During the Great Depression people lost lives, homes, and jobs. As you complete the following assignments via the World Wide Web, you will discover information on the Great Depression and its impact on our society.

Internet Resources

The Great Depression

   http://title3.sde.state.ok.us/history_and_culture/great_depression.htm   *Activities 1 & 2*

A Teacher's Guide to the Great Depression

   http://www2.blackside.com/blackside/EducationOutreach/GDguideChronology.html
   Activity 3

History of the Dust Bowl

   http://www.ultranet.com/~gregjonz/dust/dustbowl.html   *Activities 4 & 5*

Dust Bowl

   http://drylands.nasm.edu:1995/dust.html *Activities 6 & 7*

Activities

1. Farmers were very hard hit during the Great Depression. Who were the farmers growing food for and why were they unable to sell the food? What did many farmers do when they were unable to sell their food?

2. What industry was also hit hard by the Great Depression?

3. Who became President of the United States in 1929, and remained President during much of the Great Depression?

4. What states were affected by the Dust Bowl?

5. What caused the Dust Bowl?

6. What was the Dust Bowl? What caused the Dust Bowl?

7. How long did the Dust Bowl last?

Additional Activity

The Great Depression effected many lives in many ways. Use the following site to read an account of survival in the Dust Bowl:

The American Experience/Surviving the Dust Bowl

http://www.pbs.org/wgbh/pages/amex/dustbowl/interviews/glover1.html

After reading Imogene Glover's account of homesteading in the Dust Bowl, reflect on her experiences and record your thoughts for the class. If you could interview Ms. Glover, what five questions would you ask her? List your questions below.

1.

2.

3.

4.

5.

Report your findings to your class members.

Conclusion

During the Great Depression, people lost money, lives, jobs, and homes. Life was difficult during this time period, and America suffered. By reading about the life of Billie Joe and others though the World Wide Web and in books, we can learn about determination, strength, and the will to survive exhibited by our ancestors during this time in our nation's history.

Educator Notes

The Great Depression is a topic which deserves attention, as it can teach us history, economics, and personal determination. Through the use of the following Internet sites and books, additional information about the Great Depression can be found to adapt for classroom curriculum.

Websites

ALSC: John Newbery Medal—1998

http://www.ala.org/alsc/newbery.html

This is information from the Association for Library Service to Children, a division of the American Library Association.

Dear Mrs. Roosevelt

http://newdeal.feri.org/eleanor/index.htm

During the Great Depression, Mrs. Roosevelt received numerous letters from children asking for help. This web page provides an overview of the letters, how the Great Depression affected children, and lesson plans for incorporation into the curriculum.

Great Depression

http://www.globalmarketplace.com/education/nix/9.html

Presents the memories of a nine-year-old boy during the Great Depression. Includes information on the New Deal, Works Progress Administration (WPA), and Rural Electrification Administration (REA).

The Great Depression

http://204.244.141.13/writ_den/h15/direct.htm

Offers audio, quizzes, and history of the Great Depression suitable for classroom use.

Karen Hesse

http://www.ala.org/news/majorawards.html

This is the news release about the 1998 Newbery Medal winner.

Karen Hesse

http://www.riverdale.k12.or.us/~cmaxwell/hesse.htm

Provides author information and pictures of a visit Karen Hesse made to a school.

Out of the Dust

http://www.riverdale.k12.or.us/~cmaxwell/dust.htm

This is a student synopsis of the book, plus Real Audio of Karen Hesse reading selections from the book.

Overview: The Great Depression

http://www.amatecon.com/GD/gdoverview.html

Includes descriptions of family values and lifestyles and how they were affected by the Depression.

We Made Do

http://ipad.mcsc.k12.in.us/mhs/social/madedo/

This oral history page of the Great Depression is maintained by a school in Indiana. An added bonus is the ability for others to contribute oral history memories to the site. This page offers useful, first hand accounts of the Great Depression and gives students an opportunity to study the lives of others.

Books

Brug, David F. ***The Great Depression: An Eyewitness History.*** Facts on File, 1996. Includes excerpts from a variety of primary sources. Includes letters, speeches, narratives, newspaper stories, and radio accounts of from the time.

Farrell, Jacqueline. ***The Great Depression.*** Lucent, 1996. U.S. history from 1929–1945. Well-illustrated. Written for use with older children, but material is suitable for adaptation with younger students.

Fremon, David K. ***The Great Depression in American History.*** Enslow, 1997. Economic conditions during the Depression. Designed for use with children in grades 5 and up.

Nardo, Don ed. ***The Great Depression.*** Greenhaven, 1997. Presents the events of the Great Depression for children grades 4–12.

Nishi, Dennis. ***Life During the Great Depression.*** Lucent, 1997. Part of the "Way People Live Series" of books. Intended for readers in grades 4–12.

Wroble, Lisa. ***Kids During the Great Depression.*** Rosen Publishing, 1998. Children of the Depression. Includes good historical background information.

Holes

By Louis Sachar

Farrar, Straus & Giroux, 1998 • Newbery Medal, 1999

Introduction

Stanley Yelnats has had a lot of bad luck during his short life. In fact, his entire family has a history of bad luck, so it is no wonder that Stanley is sent to a strange detention center in the hot Texas desert. While there, Stanley discovers a friend, a treasure, and himself.

Assignment

After reading *Holes*, it will be time for you to embark on your own "treasure hunt." The Internet will provide the information you'll need on your treasure and how to find it.

Internet Resources

Treasure Hunting Site by Mel Fisher

    http://www.melfisher.com *Activity 1*

Museum Mania On-Line Treasure Hunt

    http://www.museummania.com/treasure.htm *Activity 2*

Drawing a Treasure Map

    http://www.jamesmdeem.com/drawa.htm *Activity 3*

Treasure Stories

    http://www.jamesmdeem.com/treasurestories.htm *Activity 4*

Burying Your Own Treasure

    http://www.jamesmdeem.com/burying.htm *Activity 5*

Activities

1. Who is Mel Fisher, and what type of treasure does he hunt for?

2. Choose a Museum Mania Treasure Hunts and complete the activity. Were you successful? Did you find treasure? What did you learn from this activity?

3. Follow the directions at this website and draw your own treasure map. Can others follow your directions ?

4. Read the treasure stories. Do you think you could find the lost treasures mentioned in the stories? What clues did you find when reading the stories? What equipment would you need to find the treasures? If you did find the lost coins or gold pieces, what would you do?

5. Read the story at this site and make a list of everything you would include in your own treasure box. Why would you include the items you chose? Where would you bury your treasure and when would you retrieve it?

Additional Activity

There are a lot of Internet treasure hunts available for you to use to practice your skills at searching the World Wide Web. Using the following address, complete the treasure hunt. Scavenger Hunt 1 is for beginners and Scavenger Hunt 2 is for experienced Internet users. Choose your category and have fun!

Internet Treasure Hunts

http://www.education-world.com/a_lesson/lesson068.shtml

Conclusion

Buried treasure can be more than objects. In the story *Holes*, one of Stanley's treasures was a new friendship. You can discover treasure in many places, people, and things.

Educator Notes

The following sources can help teachers, librarians, and parents develop units and additional LearningQuests.

Websites

Holes

http://gus82570.hypermart.net/holes.htm

This site has a short description of *Holes* along with information about Louis Sachar, who is also the author of *Dogs Don't Tell Jokes, Sideways Stories from Wayside School*, and the Marvin Redpost books.

Online Activities

http://www.csun.edu/~hcedu013/onlineactivities.html

This extensive site provides links to lots of Internet activities for children. The age level and difficulty vary, so educators will need to evaluate their selected sites. Many of the activities are Internet treasure hunts that provide children with searching skills, knowledge, and practice.

Using Treasure Hunts to Guide Your Students Through the Web

http://rkenner.concordia.ca/GSE555_98/P_Baxter/Treasure.html

Aimed at the educator, this is a report on the pros and cons of using Internet treasure hunts to promote successful use of the WWW by students. Examples of existing treasure hunts are given and a reference list.

Welcome to Museum Mania

http://www.museummania.com/index.html

Museum Mania has a nice selection of treasure hunts that are accomplished via the Web. This site also features Museum Mania literacy books, homework links, library press packets, and fund-raising ideas for libraries.

Welcome to the Newbery Medal Home Page

http://www.ala.org/alsc/newbery.html

This is the official site of the Newbery Medal where *Holes* is featured. The American Library Association sponsors the John Newbery Medal.

Yahooligans! Scavenger Hunt

http://www.yahooligans.com/content/tg/basil.html

Internet treasure hunts are a natural aid to teach searching and research skills using the World Wide Web. This site features a good plan for implementing an Internet treasure hunt with information on planning and implementing treasure hunts and creating scavenger hunts. Additional sources include assessment tools.

Books

Claybourne, Annaedt. ***Treasure Hunting.*** EDC Publishing, 1999. Buried treasure and juvenile literature combined provide many opportunities for educational extensions when using this book in a classroom.

Deem, James M. ***How to Hunt Buried Treasure.*** Houghton Mifflin, 1992. A mixture of history, speculation and fact, this book provides treasure seekers with useful information. The book gives information on types of treasure, where to find treasure, and keeping a log of treasure hunting activities.

Gallagher, Jim. ***Treasure Hunt.*** Chelsea House, 1999. The steps to finding buried treasure are adventurous and exciting. This book features some of the adventurers who have looked for the buried treasures around the world.

Hicks, Clifford B. ***Alvin's Secret Code.*** Puffin, 1998. Combine secret treasure, mysterious codes, and a detective named Alvin, and you have a good mixture for fun!

Snell, Gordon. ***Dangerous Treasure.*** Dufour Editions, 1996. Children are a natural audience for treasure, and this book provides a good look at buried treasure.

Stevenson, Robert Louis. ***Treasure Island.*** Educational Insights, 1998. This edition is just one of the many that are available for this classic book. The adventure, buried treasure, and island atmosphere make for a wonderful tale for children and adults alike.

Bud, Not Buddy
By Christopher Paul Curtis
Delacorte Press, 1999 • Newbery Medal, 2000

Introduction

Bud is ten years old and searching for his father. All he has is a suitcase of flyers, his rules for life, and a large amount of determination. Bud wants a family and his search brings him much more than he ever realized possible.

Assignment

In *Bud, Not Buddy*, family is an important theme. During this LearningQuest, you will discover information about families and genealogy. Perhaps, you may even learn more about your own family

Internet Resources

After reading this book, begin your exploration of storytelling. Think of the history of storytelling, how it has affected your life, and ways you can continue the tradition. The Internet can help you learn about storytelling, learn how to tell a story, and find stories to tell to an audience.

Word Central

http://www.wordcentral.com/ *Activity 1*

Genealogy Instructions

http://home.earthlink.net/~howardorjeff/i3.htm *Activities 2 & 3*

Questions to Ask

http://home.earthlink.net/~howardorjeff/i2.htm *Activities 4 & 5*

Activities

1. Type the work "genealogy" in the box at the tope of the page. Click "Find." What is the definition of genealogy?

2. Where are four places you can go to do genealogy research?

3. What information can you find at each research place?

4. What are three questions you can ask your family members when beginning your search about your family history?

5. Answer as many questions as you can from the list provided on this Internet page.

Additional Activity

Print the family tree from the following Internet address.

Four Generations of a Family Tree

http://www.myhistory.org/guidebook/family_tree.html

With help from family members, complete as much as the family tree as possible. Share your information with your class members.

Conclusion

In the story *Bud, Not Buddy*, Buddy Caldwell takes a trip to find a family. Most of us are fortunate that we have our families close to us. Sometimes our family consists of friends and acquaintances. Whatever your family, it has a history that you can use to learn about yourself.

Educator notes

Numerous websites provide information about families and family history. A few sites, which have been chosen for their educational value are listed below. In addition, the list includes a selection of the many books that have been published on these topics.

Websites

Genealogy for Children

http://home.istar.ca/~ljbritt/

This site provides materials designed to assist teachers, parents, and grandparents in introducing children to the exciting world of genealogy. It also provides online activities for children.

Genealogy Instructions for Beginners

http://home.earthlink.net/~howardorjeff/instruct.htm

A nice introduction to genealogy for anyone interested in starting research on their family history.

Genealogy Projects for Kids

http://home.earthlink.net/~howardorjeff/i5.htm

This site contains two genealogy activities: A Family Tree, and Photo Paste Fun.

How to Write a Family History

http://www.geocities.com/Heartland/Hills/6658/famhist.html

Contains tips for writing a family history.

I, Witness to History

http://www.iwitnesstohistory.org/

This wonderful site, developed by Larksfield Place Retirement Community, is part of a multi-faceted program designed to preserve, publish, and promote the life stories of the residents of Larksfield Place.

My Family

http://www.myfamily.com

Build a family website, report family news, share photos, build a family tree, and more at this site from MyFamily.com Inc.

My History is America's History

http://www.myhistory.org/index.html

This initiative of the National Endowment for the Humanities is designed to encourage people to explore their family histories, discover their families' place in history, and to make their own contributions to history.

Books

Davis, Donald. ***Telling Your Own Stories, A Resource for Family Storytelling, Classroom Story Creation and Personal Journaling.*** August House Publishers, 1993. Designed for anyone who wants to inspire storytelling either in themselves or in others.

Stone, Richard. ***Stories, The Family Legacy: A Guide for Recollection and Sharing.*** StoryWork Institute Press, 1994. This book assists the reader in digging out a hidden "family album" of memories, reclaiming forgotten bonds, and perhaps discovering new ones.

Stryker-Rodda, Harriet. ***How to Climb Your Family Tree: Genealogy for Beginners.*** Genealogical Publishing Company, 1995. A carefully thought-out introduction to the methods and principles of genealogical research written for the beginner.

Taylor, Mildred D. ***Song of the Trees.*** Bantam Doubleday Dell Books for Young Readers, 1996. During the Depression, a rural black family deeply attached to the forest on their land tries to save it from being cut down by an unscrupulous white man.

Marshall, Jimmie B. ***How to Record Your Family History: An Easy and Informative Guide to Writing Down and Preserve for Future Generations.*** Excelsior Cee Publishing, 1999. An easy-to-read booklet explaining the simple method of recording one's family history without the complexities of genealogical research.

LQ24

A Year Down Yonder
By Richard Peck
Dial Books for Young Readers, 2000 • Newbery Medal, 2001

Introduction

Fifteen-year-old Mary Alice leaves Chicago during the Great Depression to spend a year in a small rural town with her Grandma Dowdel. At first Mary Alice misses Chicago and is not thrilled about small towns, but she soon learns the love of her grandmother and gains love for her new life.

Assignment

Grandparents are important to our lives. During this LearningQuest, you will look at Grandparents, learn about their memories, and perhaps think of your own grandparents.

Internet Resources

National Grandparent's Day

http://www.geocities.com/Heartland/2328/grparday.htm   *Activities 1 & 2*

Family Tree

http://www.grandparents-day.com/family_tree.htm   *Activity 3*

Census Facts for Grandparent's Day

http://www.census.gov/Press-Release/fs97-09.html   *Activities 4 & 5*

Grandparent's Day Maze

http://akidsheart.com/ws/grandmaze.htm   *Activity 4*

Activities

1. When is Grandparent's Day celebrated?

2. Who originated National Grandparent's Day? Why?

3. Print and complete the family tree to the best of your ability. You may need to get help from a parent for some names. Share the results with your class.

4. Of the children living with their grandparents in 1996, how many lived just with a grandparent?

5. What percentage of the children were between the ages of 6 and 11?

6. Can you get help Grandma get her yarn to her knitting needles?

Additional Activity

Nicknames for Grandparents

http://akidsheart.com/ws/grandnamesws.htm

Try this word search activity and see how many nicknames you can find. Have fun and maybe you'll find the nickname for a special grandparent that you know!

Conclusion

Grandparents are important and can tell us a lot about ourselves. They can also tell stories of our parents when they were small children. If you have no grandparents near, why not adopt a local person to be your special grandparent? You may find yourself learning something special and enjoying a new relationship.

Educator Notes

The following sources can help teachers, librarians, and parents develop units and additional LearningQuests.

Websites

Grace Coolidge, My Grandmother

http://www.jfklibrary.org/coolidge_sayles.html

Memories of Mrs. Calvin Coolidge, as presented by her granddaughter. Calvin Coolidge was the thirtieth president of the United States, and Grace Coolidge was the first lady.

Grandparent Stories

http://www.coweta.k12.ga.us/rhes/Tallen/Stories.html

The stories about grandparents on this web page were written by young children. These stories would be a good introduction to a multilevel class activity. Older children could be paired with younger children and grandparent stories would be a good topic for discussion and writing.

Grandparent Stories

http://www.grandparentplace.com/msubstory.htm

A nice collection of stories about grandparents that could be used as examples for children writing about their own grandparents.

Grandparents and Grandchildren

http://www.geocities.com/Heartland/2328/grchild.htm

"CyberGrandma" offers advice and information for grandparents and grandchildren alike on this web page. A good site for creating curriculum extensions to a unit on grandparents.

Interview Your Grandparents

http://www.hearthsong.com/athome/projects_interview.cfm

A short series of questions is provided that can be used as interview questions for grandparents or special grandparents in the community. Children may gain a sense of history and understanding through this project.**Family Relationships**

http://parentingteens.about.com/library/weekly/aa110497.htm?once=true&

Tips and advice for building and maintaining a relationship with grandparents is presented for children and teens. Also included is a link for an article on maintaining a relationship with long distance grandparents.

National Grandparent's Day

http://www.grandparents-day.com/

The official web page of National Grandparent's Day features information on the founder, activities for celebrating National Grandparent's Day, and special events.

Books

Bawden, Nina. ***Granny the Pag.*** Clarion Books, 1996. Catriona has a grandmother who is a bit different. Her grandmother rides a motorcycle and Catriona is a bit embarrassed. But in the end, Catriona realizes just how special her grandmother really is.

Dubrovin, Vivian. ***Tradin' Tales with Grandpa: A Kid's Guide for Intergenerational Storytelling.*** Storycraft Publishing, 2001. Family storytelling is a great way to build and preserve memories. With *Tradin' Tales with Grandpa,* students will have the opportunity to learn to preserve family stories. The book would also be good for use in a classroom to extend a unit on storytelling or grandparents.

Grimes, Nikki. ***Stepping Out with Grandma Mac.*** Simon and Schuster, 2002. This poetry book describes the adventures of a grandmother and her grandchild as they take short field trips together. Told from the point of view

Lasky, Kathryn. ***True North: A Novel of the Underground Railroad.*** Scholastic Trade, 1996. Afrika is a young slave girl who is traveling the Underground Railroad. Lucy discovers Afrika in her grandfather's house, and after his death, Lucy assists Afrika on her trek to freedom.

Vaughn, Sherry T. ***Grandpa's Eyes.*** Dimensions, 1996. Grandparents can play an important role of children and this book examines that issue through the story of a grandfather and his grandson.

Newbery Medal Winners

2001	*A Year Down Yonder* (Dial Books for Young Readers)	Richard Peck
2000	*Bud, Not Buddy* (Delacorte)	Christopher Paul Curtis
1999	*Holes* (Farrar, Straus & Giroux)	Louis Sachar
1998	*Out of the Dust* (Scholastic)	Karen Hesse
1997	*The View from Saturday* (Jean Karl/Atheneum)	E. L. Konigsburg
1996	*The Midwife's Apprentice* (Clarion)	Karen Cushman
1995	*Walk Two Moons* (Harper Trophy)	Sharon Creech
1994	*The Giver* (Houghton Mifflin)	Lois Lowry
1993	*Missing May* (Orchard)	Cynthia Rylant
1992	*Shiloh* (Atheneum)	Phyllis Reynolds Naylor
1991	*Maniac Magee* (Little, Brown)	Jerry Spinelli
1990	*Number the Stars* (Houghton Mifflin)	Lois Lowry
1989	*Joyful Noise: Poems for Two Voices* (Harper & Row)	Paul Fleischman
1988	*Lincoln: A Photobiography* (Clarion)	Russell Freedman
1987	The Whipping Boy (Greenwillow)	Sid Fleischman
1986	*Sarah, Plain and Tall* (Harper)	Patricia MacLachlan
1985	*The Hero and the Crown* (Greenwillow)	Robin McKinley
1984	*Dear Mr. Henshaw* (Morrow)	Beverly Cleary
1983	*Dicey's Song* (Atheneum)	Cynthia Voight
1982	*A Visit to William Blake's Inn: Poems for Innocent and Experienced Travelers* (Harcourt)	Nancy Willard
1981	*Jacob Have I Loved* (Crowell)	Katherine Paterson
1980	*A Gathering of Days: A New England Girl's Journal, 1830 – 1832* (Scribner)	Joan W. Blos
1979	*The Westing Game* (Dutton)	Ellen Raskin

1978	*Bridge to Terabithia* (Crowell)	Katherine Paterson
1977	*Roll of Thunder, Hear My Cry* (Dial)	Mildred D. Taylor
1976	*The Grey King* (Atheneum)	Susan Cooper
1975	*M.C. Higgins, The Great* (Macmillan)	Virginia Hamilton
1974	*The Slave Dancer* (Bradbury)	Paula Fox
1973	*Julie of the Wolves* (Harper)	Jean Craighead George
1972	*Mrs. Frisby and the Rats of NIMH* (Atheneum)	Robert C. O'Brien
1971	*Summer of the Swans* (Viking)	Betsy Byars
1970	*Sounder* (Harper)	William H. Armstrong
1969	*The High King* (Holt)	Lloyd Alexander
1968	*From the Mixed-Up Files of Mrs. Basil E. Frankweiler* (Atheneum)	E. L. Konigsburg
1967	*Up a Road Slowly* (Follett)	Irene Hunt
1966	*I, Juan de Pareja* (Farrar)	Elizabeth Borton de Trevino
1965	Shadow of a Bull (Atheneum)	Maia Wojciechowska
1964	*It's Like This, Cat* (Harper)	Emily Neville
1963	*A Wrinkle in Time* (Farrar)	Madeleine L'Engle
1962	*The Bronze Bow* (Houghton Mifflin)	Elizabeth George Speare
1961	*Island of the Blue Dolphins* (Houghton Mifflin)	Scott O'Dell
1960	*Onion John* (Crowell)	Joseph Krumgold
1959	*The Witch of Blackbird Pond* (Houghton Mifflin)	Elizabeth George Speare
1958	*Rifles for Watie* (Crowell)	Harold Keith
1957	*Miracles on Maple Hill* (Harcourt)	Virginia Sorenson
1956	*Carry On, Mr. Bowditch* (Houghton Mifflin)	Jean Lee Latham
1955	*The Wheel on the School* (Harper)	Meindert DeJong
1954	*... And Now Miguel* (Crowell)	Joseph Krumgold
1953	*Secret of the Andes* (Viking)	Ann Nolan Clark
1952	*Ginger Pye* (Harcourt)	Eleanor Estes
1951	*Amos Fortune, Free Man* (Dutton)	Elizabeth Yates
1950	*The Door in the Wall* (Doubleday)	Marguerite de Angeli
1949	*King of the Wind* (Rand McNally)	Marguerite Henry
1948	*The Twenty-One Balloons* (Viking)	William Pene du Bois
1947	*Miss Hickory* (Viking)	Carolyn Sherwin Bailey

1946   *Strawberry Girl* (Lippincott) Lois Lenski

1945   *Rabbit Hill* (Viking) Robert Lawson

1944   Johnny Tremain (Houghton Mifflin) Esther Forbes

1943   *Adam of the Road* (Viking) Elizabeth Janet Gray

1942   *The Matchlock Gun* (Dodd) Walter Edmonds

1941   *Call It Courage* (Macmillan) Armstrong Sperry

1940   *Daniel Boone* (Viking) James Daugherty

1939*Thimble Summer* (Farrar and Rinehart) Elizabeth Enright

1938   *The White Stag* (Viking) Kate Seredy

1937   *Roller Skates* (Viking) Ruth Sawyer

1936   *Caddie Woodlawn* (Macmillan) Carol Ryrie Brink

1935   *Dobry* (Viking) Monica Shannon

1934*Invincible Louisa: The Story of the Author
    of* Little Women   (Little, Brown)Cornelia Meigs

1933*Young Fu of the Upper Yangtze* (Winston)   Elizabeth Lewis

1932   *Waterless Mountain* (Longmans) Laura Adams Armer

1931*The Cat Who Went to Heaven* (Macmillan)   Elizabeth Coatsworth

1930*Hitty, Her First Hundred Years* (Macmillan)   Rachel Field

1929 *The Trumpeter of Krakow* (Macmillan) Eric P. Kelly

1928*Gay Neck, The Story of a Pigeon* (Dutton)   Dhan Gopal Mukerji

1927   *Smoky, The Cowhorse* (Scribner) Will James

1926   *Shen of the Sea* (Dutton) Arthur Bowie Chrisman

1925 *Tales From Silver Lands* (Doubleday) Charles Finger

1924   *The Dark Frigate* (Little, Brown) Charles Hawes

1923*The Voyages of Doctor Dolittle* (Lippincott)   Hugh Lofting

1922   *The Story of Mankind* (Liveright) Hendrik Willem van Loon

Additional Resources

Children's Literature Websites

American Library Association
http://www.ala.org
Official site of the American Library Association. Contains many links for information on children's literature, including the following:

Book Lists from the Young Adult Library Service
http://www.ala.org/alsc/awards.html

Book Links: Connecting Books, Libraries, and Classrooms
http://www.ala.org/BookLinks

Association for Library Service to Children (ALSC)
http://www.ala.org/alsc
American Library Association committee specializing in library services for children. Contains many links to other sites that feature literature and learning activities.

The Bulletin of the Center for Children's Books
http://www.press.uillinois.edu/journals/bccb.html
Site for The Bulletin of the Center for Children's Books, a children's book review journal.

CBC Online
http://www.cbcbooks.org
Children's Book Council Web page devoted to the many aspects of children's literature

Carol Hurst's Children's Literature
http://www.carolhurst.com
Includes curriculum support for literature and book reviews. Has good ideas for incorporating good literature in the school curriculum.

Child_Lit
http://www.rci.rutgers.edu/~mjoseph/childlit/about.html
An online discussion list for those interested in research and theory of children's literature and its use with children. Postings are from librarians, teachers, parents, authors and professors.

Child Study Children's Book Committee
http://www.bnkst.edu
A World Wide Web site maintained by the Child Study Children's Book Committee at Bank Street College. This site contains useful information pertaining to the study of children and their books.

Children's Authors and Illustrators on the Web
http://www.acs.ucalgary.ca/~dkbrown/authors.html
From the Children's Literature Web Guide, an excellent resource for children's literature.

Children's Literature & Language Arts Resources
http://falcon.jmu.edu/~ramseyil/childlit.htm
Maintained by James Madison University, this site contains links for book reviews, educational sites, and numerous genre in children's literature.

Children's Literature Association
http://ebbs.english.vt.edu/chla
Neat site with nice information. This Association is devoted to the scholarly study of children's literature, and it offers links to other sites on this subject.

Children's Literature Homepage
http://www.childrenslit.com/
Contains information on children's literature and book reviews. The book reviews are written by librarians, teacher and parents.

Children's Literature Reference
http://mahogany.lib.utexas.edu/Libs/PCL/child/
Contains excellent links for children's literature, and is an electronic bibliography of children's reference resources. This site can be used as a guide for students and researchers to basic and special resources on children's literature.

Children's Literature Web Guide
http://www.ucalgary.ca/~dkbrown/
An excellent guide to Internet resources dealing with children's literature. This site contains many links, and is one of the most comprehensive sites for the study and enjoyment of children and their books. The Guide is kept current and timely.

Database of Award-Winning Children's Literature
http://www2.wcoil.com/~ellerbee/childlit.html
Choose the specific type of award winning children's book you desire. The author of this Internet resource is a librarian with an interest in children's literature.

The deGrummond Children's Literature Collection

http://www.lib.usm.edu/~degrum
A children's literature research center at the University of Southern Mississippi. The deGrummond Collection houses an Ezra Jack Keats collection.

Index to Internet Sites: Children's and Young Adults' Authors & Illustrators

http://falcon.jmu.edu/~ramseyil/biochildhome.htm
A listing of children's authors on the web. Provides useful information for an author study.

Inez Ramsey's Kids Sites: Meet the Author

http://falcon.jmu.edu/schoollibrary/kidsauthors.htm
A list of links for children's authors on the World Wide Web. This site is part of the Internet School Library Media Center.

The Internet Public Library

http://www.ipl.org
A good resource that includes a children's literature section, with information on children's books and a "story-time."

Links for Book Lovers

http://www.haemibalgassi.com/links.html
A great page featuring author links, publishers, and online bookstores.

Meet Children's Authors and Illustrators

http://www.childrenslit.com/f_mai.htm
Internet sites for numerous children's authors and illustrators.

Vandergrift's Children's Literature Page

http://www.scils.rutgers.edu/~kvander/ChildrenLit/index.html
An extensive site developed by Kay E. Vandergrift at Rutgers University. Site is continually evolving and contains excellent research on children's literature.

Yahoo!—Arts: Humanities: Literature: Genres: Children's: Authors

http://dir.yahoo.com/Arts/Humanities/Literature/Authors/Children_s/
Links for various authors of children's books.

Educational Materials Websites

American Library Association

http://www.ala.org
Official site of the American Library Association. Contains many links for educational information, including the following:

ALA Resources for Parents and Kids

http://www.ala.org/parents/

700+ Great Sites

http://www.ala.org/parentspage/greatsites/amazing.html

700+ Great Sites - Library and School Sites

http://www.ala.org/parentspage/greatsites/lib.html

For Parent and Caregivers

http://www.ala.org/alsc/parents.links.html

Learning Through the Library

http://www.ala.org/aasl/learning/
Produced by the American Association of School Librarians (AASL), this site features a best practices site, and links to learning. The AASL is a component of the American Library Association.

AskEric

http://ericir.syr.edu
Maintained by the ERIC clearinghouse for educational information. Includes many excellent and useful literature based lesson plans suitable for classroom use.

Awesome Library

http://www.awesomelibrary.org/
This site features over 12,000 links for teachers, parents, librarians, and kids. An excellent resource of information.

Blue Web'n Learning Sites Library

http://www.kn.pacbell.com/wired/bluewebn
Educational learning on the Web. Sponsored by Pacific Bell, this site links to other "Blue Ribbon" sites offering curriculum resources and activities.

Children's Literature Activities for the Classroom

http://members.aol.com/MGoudie/ChildrensLit.html
A nice site maintained by a public school teacher, this page features numerous activities that are based upon children's literature.

Classroom Connect

http://www.classroom.net
This site offers activities and product news for teachers and their students in graded K–12.

Cyberbee

http://www.cyberbee.com/
A database of lessons developed with the Internet in mind. These lessons can be used in public, private or homeschool settings.

Early Childhood Resources

http://www.monroe.k12.la.us/mcs/community/early_child/early_child.html
Numerous links designed for use with the youngest children are included in this website. A good resource for teachers, librarians and parents.

Education Place

http://www.eduplace.com
Presented by Houghton Mifflin Publishers, this site offers resources for teachers and parents, as well as a "Kid's Clubhouse" with educational games and activities.

Additional Resources

Education World
http://www.education-world.com
Featured at this site is information for all areas of education including administration, books in education, curriculum, and lesson planning. This site features a searchable database of over 110,000 Web pages.

The Global Schoolhouse
http://www.gsn.org
The Global Schoolhouse features sections for parents and teachers, kids and teens and a link for neat projects. The parent/teacher section offers information on discussion lists, resources and tools and K-12 educational opportunities.

ICONnect
http://www.ala.org/ICONN/familiesconnect.html
A site for curriculum connections and Internet resources, maintained by the American Library Association.

Internet School Library Media Center
http://falcon.jmu.edu/schoollibrary/index.html
Valuable resources for various elementary curriculum areas, professional organizations and special education.

The Internet Schoolhouse
http://www.onr.com/schoolhouse/is.html
A neat site with numerous links for all types of educational curriculum needs. This site is fun to navigate, as the main menu is a "highway" with many exits.

Kathy Schrock's Guide for Educators
http://school.discovery.com/schrockguide/
A useful educational site, loaded with many links. The categorized list of sites on the Internet are useful for enhancing curriculum and teacher professional growth. Kathy Schrock's Guide for Educators is an excellent site for those interested in the education of children.

The Mailbox
http://www.theeducationcenter.com/cgi-bin/
tec/guest.jsp
The home page for "The Mailbox" educational magazine, this site features a preview of upcoming issues and links for free educational samples.

Mustang: A Web Cruising Vehicle for Teachers
http://mustang.coled.umn.edu
From the University of Minnesota. This site simplifies searching the Web for educational resources.

Networking in the K12 Classroom
http://www.virtualschool.edu/mon/K12/index.html
Includes curriculum resources, online classrooms, teacher resource sites, professional development, and an area for children. A good site to illustrate the variety of ways the Internet can be used in the classroom.

SCORE: CyberGuides
http://www.sdcoe.k12.ca.us/score/cyberguide.html
Includes teacher guides and student activities for literature on the Internet. Sponsored by School of California, Online Resources for Education (SCORE).

TeacherLINK
http://www.teacherlink.usu.edu/
Includes links to educational Web pages, lesson plans, curriculum extenders, and subject area links. TeacherLINKS is provided by the Utah State University College of Education.

Teachers.Net
http://www.teachers.net
Chat center, lessons. reference resources, websites and networking opportunities for educators.

Books

Other useful tools for discovering information about the Internet are the following books. This bibliography is a short version of selected works that are available in many libraries or bookstores.

Benson, Allen C., and Linda M.Fodemski. ***Connecting Kids and the Internet: A Handbook for Librarians, Teachers, and Parents, 2nd Ed.*** Neal-Schuman, 1999. An extensive and useful reference. *Connecting Kids and the Internet* is a useful guide for all adults.

Campbell, Hope. ***Managing Technology in the Early Childhood Classroom***. Teacher Created Materials, 1998. Designed to help educators learn the basics of technology and integration in the classroom, this book would be a good book for the beginning learner. A nice bibliography contained in the book is an added resource for information.

Lamb, Annette C. ***Building Treehouses for Learning: Technology in Today's Classroom, 2nd Ed.*** Vision to Action, 1998. Planning effective lessons for the technology classroom.

Leu, Donald and Deborah Diadiun Leu. ***Teaching with the Internet: Lessons from the Classroom, 3rd Ed.*** Christopher-Gordon, 2000. Building on the previous titles, the third edition of this book provides the educator with lesson ideas and new approaches to technology integration. It is a practical approach for everyone, from beginner to experienced Internet user.

Lewin, Larry. ***Using the Internet to Strengthen Curriculum.*** Association for Supervision and Curriculum Development, 2001. With a focus on teaching and helping educators understand and use the Internet, this book provides information that would be useful in a classroom, school library media center, or home. Curriculum extensions include web searching, evaluation, and presentation techniques.

Offutt, Elizabeth Rhodes. ***Internet Without Fear: Practical Tips and Activities for the Elementary Classroom.*** Good Apple, 1996. From the publisher of *The Good Apple* educational journal. This book would be a good book for all interested in using the Internet in the classroom.

Pedersen, Ted, and Francis Moss. ***Internet for Kids: A Beginners's Guide to Surfin the Net.*** Price Stern Sloan, 1997. An updated version that includes a parents' and teachers' guide. Good for use in the classroom with children to aid in understanding how to search the World Wide Web.

Schrock, Kathleen. ***Evaluating Internet Web Sites: An Educator's Guide****. Master Teacher, 1997. From the author of the acclaimed educational website, this book is a good resource for the educator and parent.

appendix C

LearningQuest Template

Your LearningQuest Title Here

Introduction Assignment Internet Resources Activities Fun Things to Do
Conclusion

Introduction
State an introduction to your Learning-Quest in this space.

Assignment
You can write your task as a paragraph or in a bulleted list. The paragraph can describe the outcomes which will be attained following the completion of the LearningQuest.

- If you wish to use a bulleted list, begin here with the first step.
- Step #2.
- Continue as necessary to complete the steps for your Learning-Quest.

Internet Resources
Information about the resources the learner will use can be written here.

- <u>Link Title</u>. Describe the link to clarify if you wish. Clarify which question(s) this URL will address.
- <u>Link Title</u>. Description. Question(s)
- <u>Link Title</u>. Description. Question(s)

Activities
1. List the questions or activities which will be completed during the LearningQuest.
2. Additional questions/activities.
3. Continue or delete as required to meet objectives to answer questions or provide activities to reinforce leaning during the LearningQuest.

Fun Things to Do
This space can extend the learning process through additional activities, Internet sites or ideas. Children can draw pictures based on what they learned, complete an Internet activity or numerous other education activities.

Conclusion
A summarization of the learning can be placed here. You can also place some additional resources or Internet addresses in this space.

This page maintained by (Your name). Written, (mm/dd/yy). Last updated, mm/dd/yy.

This page adapted from the LearningQuest template written by Ru Story-Huffman, based on the WebQuest concept developed by Bernie Dodge.

LearningQuest Template With HTML Coding

<HTML> ←——————————

> Start your document here. If you do not have Web authoring software, a text only document with an .htm extension will work.

<HEAD>

<TITLE>*LearningQuest Template*</TITLE>

</HEAD>

<BODY BGCOLOR ="#ffffff">

<A NAME="Top">

<B>*Your LearningQuest Title Here*</B>

<HR><B>

<A HREF="#Introduction">Introduction</A>

<A HREF="#Assignment">Assignment</A>

<A HREF="#Internet Resources">Internet Resources</A>

<A HREF="#Questions">Questions</A>

<A HREF="#Learning Advice">Learning Advice</A>

<A HREF="#Conclusion">Conclusion</A>

<P><B><A NAME="Introduction">Introduction</A></B>

<P>*State an introduction to your LearningQuest in this space.*

<P><B><A NAME="Assignment">Assignment</A></B>

<P>*You can write your task as a paragraph or in a bulleted list. The paragraph can describe the outcomes which will be attained following the completion of the LearningQuest.*<UL>

<LI>*If you wish to use a bulleted list, begin here with the first step.*

<LI>*Step #2.*

<LI>*Step #3.*

<LI>*Continue as necessary to complete the steps for your LearningQuest.*</UL>

<P><B><A NAME="Internet Resources">Internet Resources</A></B>

<P>*Information about the resources the learner will use can be written here.*<UL>

<LI><a href="*Place full URL here*">*Place web page name here*</a>
Description (Describe the link to clarify if you wish.) Question(s) (Clarify which question(s) this URL will address.)

LearningQuest Template

\<LI>\<a href="*Place full URL here*">*Place web page name here*\</a>\
Description. Question(s)

\<LI>\<a href="*Place full URL here*">*Place web page name here*\</a>\
Description. Question(s)

\<P>\<B>\<A NAME="Questions">Questions\</A>\<OL>\</B>

\<LI>*List the questions which will be answered at the completion of the LearningQuest.*

\<LI>*Additional questions.*

\<LI>*Continue or delete as required to meet objectives to answer questions for the LearningQuest.*\</OL>

\<P>\<B>\<A NAME="Learning Advice">Learning Advice\</A>\</B>

\<P>*This space can be used to provide help for the students for use as they explore the Internet using the LearningQuest.*

\<P>\<B>\<A NAME="Conclusion">Conclusion\</A>\</B>

\<P>*A summarization of the learning can be placed here. You can also place some additional resources or Internet addresses in this space.*

\<HR>This page maintained by *(Your name)*. Written, *(mm/dd/yy)*. Last updated, *(mm/dd/yy)*. http://www.*yourURL/YourDocumentName*.htm\</B>

\<A HREF="#Top"> Top of Page

\</BODY>

\</HTML> ⟵ This should be the last element in your document.

Note: Italics indicate where your text should be placed. Use plain text for your inserted information, italics are here only to indicate where new text should be added.

When you have finished your LearningQuest, you can test it in your Web browser. If you do not have Web authoring software, select the Open File option from the File pulldown menu. Different browsers will render type differently. If you are using LearningQuests on a single type of computer with one browser you can get more creative with type and graphics without losing control of the way your document appears on screen.

You can also find an electronic version of this template at:

Template page for *Newbery on the Net*
www.hpress.highsmith.com/rsh1up.htm